Science, Religion, and Health

Science, Religion, and Health

The Interface of Psychology and Theology/Spirituality

J. HAROLD ELLENS

Foreword by F. MORGAN ROBERTS
Afterword by H. NEWTON MALONY

CASCADE *Books* • Eugene, Oregon

SCIENCE, RELIGION, AND HEALTH
The Interface of Psychology and Theology/Spirituality

Copyright © 2016 J. Harold Ellens. All rights reserved. Except for brief quotations in critical publications or reviews, no part of this book may be reproduced in any manner without prior written permission from the publisher. Write: Permissions, Wipf and Stock Publishers, 199 W. 8th Ave., Suite 3, Eugene, OR 97401.

Cascade Books
An Imprint of Wipf and Stock Publishers
199 W. 8th Ave., Suite 3
Eugene, OR 97401

www.wipfandstock.com

PAPERBACK ISBN: 978-1-5326-0176-7
HARDCOVER ISBN: 978-1-5326-0178-1
EBOOK ISBN: 978-1-5326-0177-4

Cataloging-in-Publication data:

Names: Ellens, J. Harold, 1932– | Roberts, F. Morgan. | Malony, H. Newton

Title: Science, religion, and health : the interface of psychology and theology/spirituality / J. Harold Ellens ; foreword by F. Morgan Roberts ; afterword by H. Newton Malony.

Description: Eugene, OR: Cascade Books. | Includes bibliographical references and index.

Identifiers: ISBN: 978-1-5326-0176-7 (paperback) | 978-1-5326-0178-1 (hardback) | 978-1-5326-0177-4 (ebook)

Subjects: LCSH: Pastoral theology. | Theology, Practical. | Intercultural communication.

Classification: BR110 E45 2016 (print) | BR110 (ebook)

Manufactured in the U.S.A. NOVEMBER 8, 2016

Dedication

Beuna Coburn Carlson
Builder with me in the Cause
of the Kingdom of God in the Earth
Co-Creator of Beauty
Like God, an Aesthete

John Tracey Greene
Soldier: Comrade in Arms in the U.S. Army
Professor: Compatriot in the Scholarship of Biblical Studies
Archeologist: Co-laborer in Digging up the Truth
Author: Colleague in Articulating the Truth which Makes us Free
Courageous in all Things
Carrying on Valiantly

Contents

Foreword by F. Morgan Roberts | ix

1. Reflections on Human Health | 1
2. Spirituality, Religion, and Science: Principles and Possibilities | 11
3. Interface of Psychology and Theology | 26
4. Anxiety and the Rise of Religious Experience | 40
5. The Biblical-Theological Underpinnings | 54
6. The Psychodynamics of the Fall Story | 68
7. Modern Notions of Human Nature | 81
8. Consequences for Psychotherapy | 93
9. Concluding Observations: Transference and Countertransference | 104

Afterword by H. Newton Malony | 111

Bibliography | 115

Index | 121

Foreword

THERE IS A VAST amount of learning packed into this relatively small volume to which I wish I had been introduced before completing my seminary education in 1953. That very date should tell you that, during my seminary years, there was not such a strong connection between theology and psychology as there is today. The required courses of study indicate that we were being trained principally to be preachers and not counselors. Homiletics and speech courses were required every year and, in addition to the courses, we attended weekly practice preaching sessions in which a student's sermon would receive an appraisal (often deservedly painful) by both the homiletics and speech professors.

In contrast to those homiletical requirements, an elective course in pastoral psychology was taught by a visiting professor, a working pastor who had acquired credentials in that discipline. Understandably, those of us who faced a future in which we would have to deliver a sermon almost every Sunday for the remaining years of our ministerial career did not take that course. We went forth to our first church devoid of the skills in pastoral care with which today's seminary graduates are equipped. With our slender equipment we did our best. Whether in hospital visitation or in painful situations in which our members sought counsel we did what we could. Hopefully, we learned to be compassionate listeners; however, some of us may have resorted to giving advice, maybe even bad advice. Maybe even some of us, after a few years, learned our limitations, and began referring persons with serious problems to trained therapists. One blessing for our needy members was that pastoral care and counseling did not consume the largest part of our workweek.

Our "big thing" was the sermon; as each Sunday came relentlessly around, we had to preach the word, and in doing this we were "doing theology." If we didn't do much psychology, we did lots of theologizing. And it is in this part of the pastoral task that all pastors need the central message of this fine little volume. I say that because many of us mounted the pulpit every Sunday without the awareness that, even if we weren't skilled counselors in helping our people out of their illnesses, our theology may have been driving them even deeper into psychospiritual sickness. We did not realize that the theological content our preaching, which had been acquired in our home church, and remained untouched by our seminary education, was not health-giving. We did not realize that sick theology makes people sick.

What J. Harold Ellens makes clear from the outset in this book (and in almost every book he has ever written) is that nothing less than a clear theology of radical, unconditional, and universal grace can create the wholeness that God desires for all people. Maybe I missed it as I wrestled inwardly with the documentary hypothesis, but I cannot remember anything from my seminary studies that opened my eyes to this grand central truth as it arises in the Yahwist tradition and makes its way through (some) psalms and the prophets (especially Second Isaiah) and comes to full expression in life and ministry of Jesus. How much more life-giving my ministry might have been if, from the outset, I had "done theology" in light of God's radical grace.

There is much more to be learned in this book, but the heart of the matter is clear. There is an amazing grace out of which we can never fall. There is a love that will never let us go. Ministry informed by such a theology enhances human psychological and spiritual health.

F. Morgan Roberts
Louisville Presbyterian Theological Seminary

1

Reflections on Human Health

THINKING ABOUT HUMAN HEALTH is a stimulating and mystifying matter. It stimulates the mind, drawing one into the marvelous scope and variety of human life and function, as one begins to realize that the issue of health touches and takes in most of the experience of being human. It is immediately apparent not only that one must always be either healthy or unhealthy in body, mind, and psyche, but also that there are an incredible number and quality of ways in which one can be sick or well. Yet it is impressive that those ways in which humans get sick tend to fall into very stereotyped patterns. From that point of view, the number and variety of ways people can be pathological seems finite, typical, and relatively predictable.

On the other hand, we have our own individualized style of being ill or well, that is, of reacting to, managing, or carrying our health and/or our illness. We are so typically human and yet so surprisingly unique, for better or for worse, in sickness and in health. Likewise getting well can usually be achieved in surprisingly prescribed ways, yet each human does it with an intriguing distinctiveness. That is why it is also mystifying to speak of human health. Humans are or are not healthy so remarkably variously; and as if that did not sufficiently complicate the matter of what health is and how it is achieved, the variety of definitions of health in professional literature and in the popular mind is legion.

I remember I was fourteen when I first came genuinely to grips with the issue of what health is. It was during my sophomore year in high school. The quest was stimulated by a rather wide-ranging course in general biology. I was a small, rather neurotic, withdrawn, intense, and anxiety-laden, shy, pubescent boy. I was at least semi-conscious of the fact that I was maturing extremely late. I am not certain whether the painfulness of body and psyche that seemed to dominate my experience is typical for early adolescence, whether it was mainly physical or psychological, or whether it was healthy at the time. What I do remember is that it stimulated my thinking about health at the same time that it mystified me.

The quest came rather quickly to something helpful: an applied definition of health. I have no idea which supplemental text we were using. It may have been one of those weekly student journals that were so popular in schools at the time. In any case, it simply said that health is the state or condition in which a person can carry out a normal pattern or program of work without experiencing inappropriate pain. The teacher was impressed that I had caught that. I was astonished that no other student had. The teacher was suffering from a chronic illness, and the other students were rather robust and beyond puberty. Perhaps need prompted me to fix on the issue, which for the others had not come to mind.

Since then I have found that two things are true about health. First, most of us take it for granted when we have it. Second, this elementary definition is the best place to begin thinking about health. In this day of increasing emphasis upon holistic health care, the old positivist notion that health is essentially, if not exclusively, a matter of physical well-being, seems to be receding. Few professionals would now argue with the notion that health is more than physical well-being. Most readily agree that health involves also the interrelatedness of physical, mental, and social well-being. Even in the popular mind the holistic notion is genuinely gaining ground. These gains have been a long time in developing.

In ancient societies of the Near East from 3200 BCE to 1000 CE—in the cultures from which the West draws its sources and resources—Egyptian, Mesopotamian, Hebrew, Greek, and Roman—the stress was on physical well-being and prescriptions for physical hygiene. Matters that would be referred to today as mental hygiene or psychotherapy were largely related to the realm of religion. Emphasis upon physical health continued through the Renaissance and well into the eighteenth century. Horace Mann, first secretary of the board of education in the United States, emphasized as late as 1840 that educating for health as physical well-being was crucial.

In 1850 Lemuel Shattuck, in his *Report on the Sanitary Conditions of Massachusetts*, emphasized the need for preventive programs of disease control, indicating that health was more than the absence of disease. However, his orientation remained essentially shaped by the physical emphasis.

There were notable exceptions to this over the centuries. Already in Homeric times Asklepios in sixth-century Greece, and more specifically Hippocrates in the fifth-century Athens, placed considerable emphasis upon both physical and spiritual well-being, that is, on the health of *soma* and *psyche*. This emphasis was weaker in the Roman, Galen, since he focused more on the exclusively physical and not so much on the psychological and spiritual components of health and disease. In the early modern period it surfaced briefly in John Locke's emphasis (*The Locke Reader*). He considered "a sound mind in a sound body" to be essential.

It was only after the two world wars of the twentieth century that notions of health as optimal well-being in body, mind, and relationships began to take palpable form. Out of that development came such definitions of health as the following.

1. Health is a state of complete physical, mental, and social well-being and not merely the absence of disease or infirmity.
2. Health is that complete fitness of body, soundness of mind, and wholeness of emotions that make possible the highest quality of effective living and service.
3. Health is the quality of life, resulting from the total functioning of the individual, that empowers him or her to achieve a personally satisfying and socially useful life.
4. Health is the condition under which the individual is able to mobilize all his or her resources—intellectual, emotional, and physical—for optimal living.

Such holistic axioms take seriously the health-impacting significance of total personhood and do not underestimate the role that social relationships play in enhancing or defeating health. By the mid-twentieth-century the goal of health called not only for the cure or alleviation of disease. It called for even more than the prevention of disease. Rather it looked beyond, to strive for maximum physical, mental, and social efficiency for the individual, his or her family, and for the community.

The value of this perspective, as is generally recognized today, lies in the fact that it considers health in positive rather than negative terms. Health is not merely disease control, cure, or prevention. It is the achievement of a high level of wellness for all in the human community and for the community and its environment as a living organism. Health is a dynamic process, not a static state. It is a life quality into which humans grow on a continuum that reaches ever forward and upward, rather than a status which people can achieve and at which they can then lie dormant or quiescent.

Hence it becomes less significant to speak of healthy or unhealthy, and more meaningful to speak of relative levels of wellness. Physical, mental, and social well-being interact causatively and dynamically on the continuum from minimal to optimal wellness, as seen by most professionals and laity in the helping professions today.

A simple and direct link may be seen between the definition of health I encountered in 1946 and this holistic notion of health. Health as freedom from disease or pain is a notion that has in it the seeds of the definitions of health by J. F. Williams (2). He asserted that health is that quality of life that enables the individual to live most and serve best. Such a quality of life, instead of mere quantity of physical freedom from disease, inevitably includes the holistic concerns of body, mind, and spirit. Williams emphasizes that the health needs of persons correspond to those of nations: vigor, vitality, progress toward a better way of life, and absorption in the pursuit of objective causes that enhance growth in quality.

This emphasis on the intricate relationship between health and growth is crucial for understanding the primary concern of this book about the relationship between authentic spirituality, wholesome religion, and holistic human health. Since Francis Bacon's revival and elaboration of Aristotle's controlled scientific method, the modern era has thought about nearly everything, especially the exact and applied sciences, in cause-effect terms. That outlook and its inherent confidence in the human ability to identify, analyze, and solve problems in the world of physical reality has been a great boon to the development of health care and the medical sciences.

The techniques for employing the causative perspective in health care have evolved rapidly. The nineteenth century saw a cause-effect model that largely identified a single effect in human health and illness with a single cause, and vice versa. By 1920, following World War I, a second model was in vogue, taking a more comprehensive approach, recognizing the multiplicity of cause-and-effect factors influencing wellness and illness in humans. A solid advance was evident in epidemiology as regards recognition of the interactive forces in the multiple causes and effects. The social-ecological model had been born in which disease, for example, was seen to be the result of the condition of the host, plus the environment, and personal factors. The rise of Freudian psychology, replacing the old faculty psychology of the nineteenth century, was not insignificant in this development.

Since World War II and the rise of the World Health Organization (WHO), the multiple cause and multiple effect notion of illness and wellness has reached a relatively sophisticated level, taking with great seriousness the role of social, psychological, and physiological phenomena in shaping the health of humans and, incidentally, of most of the higher animals. By the ushering in of the twenty-first century, health concerns and agencies have globalized this multiple cause—multiple effect model. The Center for Disease Control and comparable agencies of other countries have joined forces with WHO to attack everything from AIDS to Ebola, Malaria, Small Pox, malnutrition, Zika, and other international threats to our health.

By 1970 in the United States, the effects of John F. Kennedy's emphasis upon the high-level wellness model, implemented by individual responsibility for exercise, nutrition, stress management, and control of harmful substances, was well entrenched. The decades of the 1980s and 90s built predictably on that with the working out of the President Johnson's Great Society Era and the reach toward the turn of the millennium. Americans became increasingly aware of ecology issues and their relationship to holistic health for persons and world society, as did the populations of nations around the world. We have grown an increasing emphasis upon measurement of wellness quality and efforts to calculate the manner and degree to which that is shaped by manageable planning. We are now aware of the way all that is shaped by environmental and social-psychological as well as specifically medical conditions. All these have a bearing on relationships, self-image, and the will to health. The objective is obviously to quantify the variable factors and so enhance control of illness-and-wellness-inducing dynamics.

The post-modern era has brought to us, in the last two decades, a serious distrust of empirical science as the channel to full holistic health. In consequence it has given us an interesting side effect of this increased awareness and search for new methods of health care that I have just described. We have seen a great expansion of the alternative medicine and nutritional supplements components of holistic health care concerns. This has very recently included serious research at Johns Hopkins University, New York University, and Harvard University on the therapeutic effects of cannabis, psychedelic substances, and entheogens (Ellens 2014). The prospects for these to enter the standard field of approved pharmacology seem quite positive.

So we see that over the decades of the twentieth century, and on into the twenty-first, a considerable number of advances have been made in development of the constantly improving models of health. Early in that process, as we have seen, was the recognition of the triad of interacting agents of body, mind, and spirit, *intrinsic* to humans and to health.

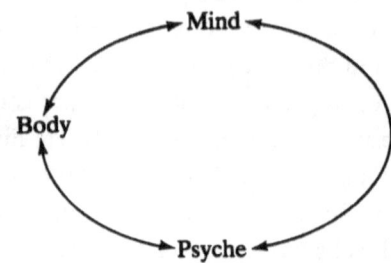

Figure 1.

A substantial step beyond that came with the recognition that a triad of forces *extrinsic* to human beings also shaped human health: host factors, environmental social factors, and personal behavior factors.

Figure 2. The Social Ecological Model

```
   Genetic                                          Physical
          \      HOST         EXTERNAL       /
           \   FACTORS      ENVIRONMENTAL   /
            \                  FACTORS     /
   Experiential                              Social

                        PERSONAL
                        BEHAVIOR
                        FACTORS
```

SOURCE: Adapted from J. N. Morris, *Uses of Epidemiology*, 3rd ed. (Edinburgh: Churchill Livingstone, 1975), p. 177.

With the advent of the WHO, holistic influence in the world emphasizing that health is a state of complete physical, mental, and social well-being and not merely the absence of disease or infirmity, the social ecological model was elaborated fully and integrated into the world Environment of Health Model.

Figure 3. The Environment of Health Model

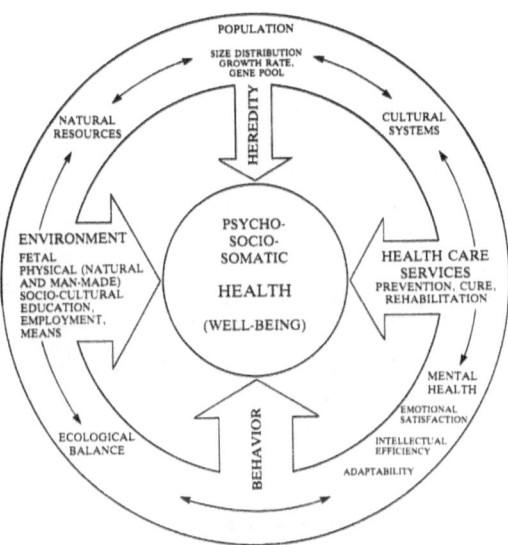

The width of the four large input-to-health arrows indicates assumptions about the relative importance of the inputs to health. The four inputs are shown as relating to and affecting one another by means of an encompassing matrix which could be called the "environment" of the health system.

SOURCE: H. L. Blum, *Planning for Health—Developmental Application of Social Change Theory* (New York: Human Sciences Press, 1974), p. 3.

The width of the four large input-to-health arrows indicate assumptions about the relative importance of those inputs to health. The four inputs are shown as relating to and affecting one another by means of the encompassing matrix which could be called the "environment" of the health system. In this model the holistic emphasis may be defined as concern with the whole person's growth toward intrinsic and extrinsic harmony and homeostasis. It means that the health care process is a matter of treating people, not diseases.

Blum, Lalonde, and Dever are now famous for this holistic emphasis. Lalonde speaks of it as the Health Field Concept.

Figure 4. The Health Field Concept

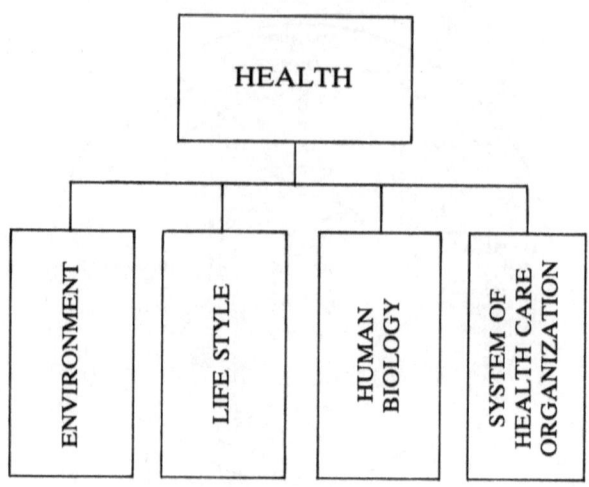

SOURCE: M. Lalonde, *A New Perspective on the Health of Canadians* (Ottawa: Office of the Canadian Minister of National Health and Welfare, April 1974), p. 31.

In figure 5 Dever's Epidemiological Model elaborates Lalonde's

Figure 5. An Epidemiological Model for Health Policy Analysis

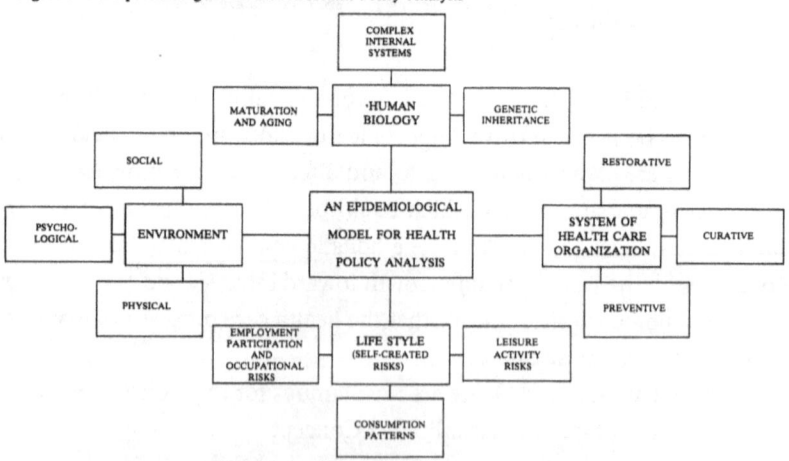

SOURCE: G. E. Alan Dever, "An Epidemiological Model for Health Policy Analysis," *Social Indicators Research* 2, p. 455, 1976. Reprinted by permission from D. Reidel Publishing Company, Dordrecht, Holland.

Thus the matter is carried well beyond the notion of health as the cure or elimination of diseases that cause illness. Health is now defined in terms of increasing degrees of conditions of wellness, as indicated in Travis' Illness/Wellness Continuum.

Figure 6. Illness/Wellness Continuum

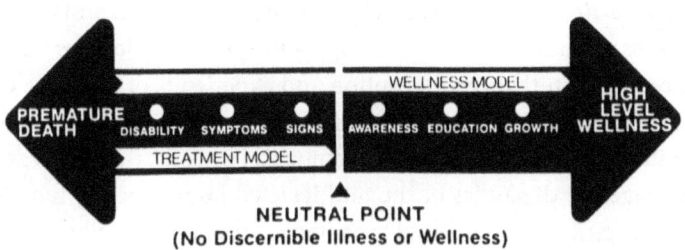

SOURCE: Reprinted with permission from *Wellness Workbook,* by Regina Ryan and John Travis, M.D., published by Ten-Speed Press, 1981.

We have advanced significantly from my insight at fourteen to truly holistic models. However, already in the notion that health is the state or condition in which a person can carry out a normal pattern or program of work without experiencing inappropriate pain lies the conceptual sources for the comprehensive definition of holistic health.

This book intends to urge one crucial additional dimension to the whole matter: the crucial significance for human health of a person's relationship to God. *Science, Religion, and Health* contends that a person's actual ontological relationship with God, as well as his or her perceived relationship, definitively affects the quality or state of that person's health. Sometimes the "posture before the face of God" is of such a sort that it creates or expands pathology. Sometimes that real or perceived relationship enhances health in body, mind, and psyche.

The thesis of this book is not a new invitation to the self-defeating processes of spiritism or the occult. It is very much the opposite. It is a claim for the notion that holistic health involves the self-actualization in persons of the full range of grand potentials for growth in body (*soma*), mind (*nous*), psyche (*psyche*), and spirit (*pneuma*) with which God has invested humans by creating us in God's own image.

Health in this book, therefore, must be defined as that state or condition in which a person is achieving or has achieved the quality of life that arises out of a full-orbed realization/actualization of all the physical, spiritual, psychological, and mental possibilities with which God has invested humans and humanness. The crucial words are, therefore, growth, dynamics, potential, and wellness, which stand behind and are implied in that definition.

Science, Religion, and Health claims that both the science of the helping professions and the science of theology and spirituality lead us uniformly to the recognition that the perception and experience of God as a God of grace is the central healing dynamic in human health. There is no magic in that. It urges rather a sound rational empirical investigation of measurable and manageable dynamics of the multifaceted human being, functioning optimally: spiritually, mentally, psychologically, and physically.

2

Spirituality, Religion, and Science: Principles and Possibilities

FOR MORE THAN HALF a century a dialogue has prevailed in the helping professions in America regarding the relationship of psychology and theology or spirituality. Surprisingly this conversation has surfaced nowhere else in the world except Brazil where the American experiment was transplanted some thirty years ago. The dialogue has been characterized as an endeavor to understand the interface or integration of the two scientific enterprises: psychology and issues of theology, spirituality, and religion. It demonstrates a serious concern about the relationship between faith and life.

On the theoretical level it concerns the question of the essential nature of science. On the practical level it concerns the question of responsible discipleship in applied disciplines. The enterprise seems pregnant with new insights, new routes across the frontiers of the sciences of both theology and psychology, and new potentials for doing both theological and psychological sciences more wisely and creatively at the theoretical and applied levels. The motivation driving the dialogue is the Christian conviction that there is a necessary, rather than accidental, relationship between being an imager and celebrator of God as a God of grace, on the one hand, and being a psychological scientist and therapist on the other.

There are difficulties inherent in this matter. One is the matter of basic definitions. In his book, *Mind and Madness in Ancient Greece*, Bennett Simon declared that the difficulty in talking about psychology is that of getting a commonly agreed upon definition of it, even among specialists in psychology. Difficulties of definition have complicated the dialogue for much of the last century. The complexities of summarizing such theoretical constituents of the dialogue as sound theories of personality and pathology is one of the problems. Achieving a responsible faith-centered critique and appreciation of classical psychological formulations and models, such as those of Freud, James, Adler, Jung, Maslow, Rogers, Sullivan, Piaget, Winnecott, Fromm, Frankl, Lacan, Fowler, Seligman, Drewermann, Capps, and the like, is also a major complexity.

This chapter is an overview of that dialogue and those complexities. It addresses (1) the central problem, (2) two principles involved, (3) eight possibilities, and (4) twelve practical applications as a preview of our investigation of spirituality, religion, and health. The central problem is rooted in the difficulty regarding the name given to the conceptual model that has developed over the decades of the dialogue's development. It has been referred to as the model of integration of psychology and theology, the model of interface between psychology and theology, and what I call the illumination model of psychology and theology. Satisfactory models or paradigms are usually difficult to construct. To work well they must be articulate of the purpose of the paradigm, comprehensive of the details, and accurate in their description of what they are trying to accomplish. The way faith relates to science, or Christian perspective to psychological theory and therapeutic practice is surely far from self-evident.

Arthur Holmes contends that there are three ways science and religion relate. (Holmes, 1971).

1. Both are models for explaining reality.

2. Conflict between them is never ultimately about empirical data but about *a priori* principles or philosophical assumptions: faith commitments.

3. Properly conceived, all science, as all human experience, finds its ultimate meaning in religion: the perspective of a faith commitment.

Nicholas Wolterstorff essentially agrees, but presses harder the fact that all scientific theory formulation is born in the first place, out of one's religious and theological predisposition. All the data one acquires is, therefore, not strictly speaking empirical data or objective rationality but rather formulations of *Reason Within the Bounds of Religion* (Wolterstorff).

Both observations help to focus the problematic issue rooted in the name of the conceptual model: integration, interface, or illumination. The model that assumes that the relationship between psychology and theology is a matter of integrating the two into each other, suggests two disparate entities, psychology and theology, essentially alien or in tension with each other, which must be lined up or force-fitted to each other in order to insure a responsible outcome in academic and clinical or pastoral activity. This is an epistemological problem on the theoretical science level, a structural problem on the applied science level, and a problem of psychodynamic dissonance on the experience level.

It is a problem because the integration model is an inaccurate picture of reality on two counts. First, it holds at its base the essentially American fundamentalist notion that truth comes only through the Christian scriptures, by the special revealing action of the Holy Spirit of God. Such a view devalues God's general revelation in the world studied by the natural and social sciences. That is, the name, *integration*, suggests that science, our reading of God's book of nature, is at war with the Christian religion, namely, our reading of God's other book, the Holy Bible.

That notion is a left over of the schizoid way apocalyptic fundamentalism sets the natural and supernatural worlds at odds. It demarcates the domain of God and of the demonic and sets them in opposition to each other. An unbiblical assumption lies at the bottom of this dichotomy. It implies that God does not live here but must invade alien territory to enter the domain of "this world" and its arena of scientific truth. Scholars who stand more consciously in the historic tradition of the Reformation should know very well that God lives here, but give the distinct impression that they are not sure God's living here really makes that much difference. The integration model has in it a further problem because it tends to imply that effective Christian life in the helping professions requires absorbing psychology into theology or absorbing theology into psychology.

Some of the literature about the integration model implies that psychology and theology remain aliens to be aligned but never really integrated; disparate fields to be worked in by individual psychologists and believers, but not quite a place for either to be at home. One gets the impression that in so far as Christians feel at home in psychology while retaining their faith commitment, they do so by forcing psychological notions into their Christian belief categories and proceeding as through the science of psychology has no prerogatives of its own. One is either a psychologist who happens incidentally to be a believer and hence a kind of lay theologian with a Sunday School level of theology, or one is a theologian who happens incidentally to be thoughtful in a kind of "pop psych" sense.

When we speak of the interface of psychology and theology we are suggesting, instead, that each of these is a domain of inquiry that has its own perspective and universe of discourse, but the two of them have the same subject matter, namely, the human person. Thus, the illumination model is closely connected to this and may be thought of as an elaboration of the interface model. It is focused upon the degree to which, and the manner in which, psychology and theology, as independent sciences, bring to each other's research the illumination that each has to offer to a comprehensive perspective on the human person, what Boisen called, the Living Human Document.

The critical assumption behind the two related models is that the worlds of materiality and spirituality are God's worlds of reality in which God's truth in revealed in the sciences of theology and psychology, as well as in the experience of piety or spirituality. What we learn from the material and spiritual universes by scientific inquiry is God's truth. All truth is God's truth about nature and grace. All truth that we learn by our inquiry into and achievement of understanding of our worlds of experience is God's revelation to us.

TRUTH FROM SCIENCE

Theology and psychology are both sciences in their own right, stand legitimately on their own foundations, and read carefully are the two books of God's revelation. They are not alien in any inherent sense. When they seem paradoxical or disparate, it must always be because of dysfunction on one of three counts. First, the professional studying them has failed to read the Bible well enough. Second, the scientist has failed to discern clearly enough the nature of the created world. Third, the investigator has distorted the science of either theology or of the material and social world. This latter is often the result of imposing ideological perspective upon the scientific process or by arbitrary dogmatism, not properly constrained by sound investigation of God's word in creation or scripture. The process may also be corrupted by drawing erroneous conclusions on either of the investigations.

Wherever truth is disclosed it is always God's truth (Holmes, 1977). Whether it is found in general revelation (mundane, material/social world) or special revelation (the sacred scriptures of religious communities), it is truth which has equal warrant with all other truth. Some truth may have greater importance than other truth, or greater urgency and application to a specific situation than other truth, but there is no difference in a truth from the Bible, Qur'an, or Upanishads, in its warrant as *truth*.

I have witnessed Evangelical Christians claim that because Carl Rogers had left his evangelical moorings years ago, his contribution to scholarship was not shaped and infused by the Holy Spirit, and therefore his insights regarding psychological dynamics and therapy could be of no value or usefulness to the Christian scientist or practitioner. Apparently, in such a framework of thought, the Christian and secularist do not differ merely in philosophical perspective and in ways of integrating their scientific insights into their world views. They differ in that the scientific endeavor of each in theology and psychology amounts to their practicing different kinds of science in both areas of study.

Some evangelical psychologists tend to absorb all of psychology into their theology. This tragedy is compounded by their erroneous theology which is not rooted in God's radical, unconditional, uncalculating, and universal grace, as made clear in Paul's Epistle to the Romans and in the Gospel of John, as well as innumerable citations in the Hebrew Bible, and Sacred Scriptures of other faith traditions. The concept and model of integration must be dispensed with, in favor of the interface and illumination models, lest the fundamentalist absorbs psychology into his or her theology; and the secularist absorbs theology into his or her psychology.

The real issue in the quest for Christian responsibility in the helping professions is the search for a method and model of employing theology from a psychological perspective and employing psychology from a theological perspective. That perspectival model of theoretical and applied professional work, allows for taking seriously the legitimacy of both sciences, and acknowledging in operational models that both sciences are generically one, unified, and not mutually alien. The *perspectival* model assumes the universal lordship of God in all things, and the source of all truth, as Philo Judaeus claimed in the time of Christ.

TWO PRINCIPLES

There are two principles that must be taken seriously in laying the groundwork for the perspectival model. The *first principle* regards what constitutes the distinctiveness of being Christian in the helping professions. In the realm of psychological theory development, the first principle of being Christian is not that our scientific achievement supports, reinforces, or coordinates with our theology or faith perspective, but that it reflects God's truth from the created world in our science. To be distinctively Christian requires that psychological theory development produce warrantable scientific theory. In the realm of psychological practice, the first principle of being Christian is not that the therapy conforms to our theology, but that it is the most superbly sound psychotherapy possible. To be a Christian therapist requires first of all that one be a thoroughly effective therapist. Otherwise one may be both a Christian of sorts and a therapist of sorts but not yet a Christian therapist.

Sound psychological theory and practice genuinely enhances the patient's progress from pathology to full-orbed personhood. God designed what that is. Christians perceive it in varying degrees. Full-orbed personhood may be achieved by patients to varying levels of completeness or functionality. Sound psychology which brings the patient out of depression to emotional resilience and stability is just as Christian as is bringing a person to the health of mature spiritual meaning and wholeness. Even if the deliverance of a patient from illness is done by a secular therapist, it is God's deliverance of that suffering person and thus a Christian enterprise, even though it may never achieve the psychospiritual completeness it could under a comparably effective Christian therapist.

What makes practice in the helping professions Christian is less the imparting of biblical information or religious practices to the patient, and more the enhancement of healthy functionality of the human as person in the direction of wholeness in body, mind, and spirit. That practice of the helping professions that is preoccupied with the final step of wholeness, namely spiritual maturity, will usually short-circuit the therapeutic process and play the religious dynamic of the patient or therapist straight into the typical religious patient's psychopathology. Such practice tends to reinforce, for example, the constipated anger, low self-esteem, compulsivity, or psychotic decision-making of the schizophrenic patient and his or her tendency toward exchanging the real world for a psychotic one.

The *second principle* regarding being a Christian in the helping professions is the necessity of the incarnational style of the professional therapist. As in all forms of incarnation, that of Jesus supremely so—that man with a life full of God, the import and impact of the role is more direct and life shaping for the incarnating one than for the object of that person's ministry or service.

The Christian therapist fills the role of incarnating for the patient the healing expectation, direction, and certification from a Christian perspective. The requirements of incarnating the healing power and technique directly shape the therapist; conditioning the therapist's values, attitudes, goals, insights, techniques, and passions in terms of the divine claims of sound science and sound faith. The impact upon the client is indirect. Being a Christian psychologist has more to do with what is happening in the therapist's attitude, thought, experience, and professional and personal quality than it has to do with what happens to the patient. The impact upon the patient should manifest itself in the way the Christian therapist's perspective and nature seep through the work into the patient's experience of the therapist's quality as a person and as a professional. The therapist's patient-handling technique and expectations regarding what health means must incarnate sound Christianity and sound science. Perhaps ultimately the impact desired is that of the therapist's world view seeping into the patient's experience.

EIGHT POSSIBILITIES

The eight possibilities for shaping the therapist's development for the incarnational role as a Christian in the helping professions are eight biblical themes. The themes ought to be incorporated into the Christian professional's conceptualization of life and work. The themes are the biblical concepts of personhood, alienation, grace, sin, discipline, "the wounded healer", mortality, and celebration as a way of life. The biblical concepts ring true to and illumine psychological theory and practice at key points. Biblical anthropology illumines sound psychosocial research.

The *biblical theology of personhood* is surprising and profound. Unconditional grace theology is clearly the central biblical theme from the text tradition of the Yahwist in the Pentateuch, properly read and critiqued, through the Psalms of grace, to the covenant theology of some of the prophets such as Hosea and Micah, Isaiah, Zechariah and Malachi, the Fourth Gospel, and Paul's Epistles. In that entire literary fabric one thing is overwhelmingly clear. Human persons are unconditionally cherished by God, in spite of themselves. God so loved the world that God created it. God made humans inherently imagers of God's self. God invested all persons with unnegotiable and inviolable dignity, from the outset imparting to each the status of compatriot of God. The myth of Eden does not speak of humanity as children, servants, or subordinates of God, but depicts humanity as divine compatriots. God visited them in the cool of the evening, they shared God's enterprises of keeping the garden and naming the animals. Humanity was placed in a complimentary relationship with God.

That imputed status was never abrogated, despite the human declaration of independence, under the threat of death. God's response to humanity's stumble into adolescence was to change the ground rules at God's expense and reaffirm humankind's dignified status and destiny as co-laborers in building God's world. In that inviolable status every person has only two potential conditions: to be in a posture that rings true to that God-given status and therefore true to self, or to be inauthentic in perspective, disposition or behavior, and suffer the dissonance and dis-ease inherent to that lack of authenticity.

Through it all, God remains preoccupied with human need, not human naughtiness, with human failure of destiny more than that of duty, and with the redeemed potential, not with the sinful past. If God confirms patients and therapists in that quality of personhood, Christian psychological theory and practice must be based upon it. Patients are free to be what they are for the sake of what they can become, before the face of God.

The *biblical theology of alienation* is described by Paul when he asserts that all have fallen short of the glorious destiny God envisions for humanity. The Bible describes humans as children who have lost touch with the Father's hand, so to speak. Aurelius Augustine described the condition in his pathetic personal prayer, "Thou has made us for thyself, and our souls are restless until they rest, O God, in thee."

The brokenness of humanity is obvious. Its psychological consequences are evident every day everywhere. We have not overcome our shortfall, as Paul said. We are not far enough yet from the Chimpanzee. The brokenness and disjointedness of the psyche of all humans is empirical expression of the human longing for a Father's hand, and the primal anxiety permeating everything because we cannot catch hold of it. We all thirst for life's spiritual anxiety reduction. The many compensatory strategies incited by all that, are frequently additional dynamics that produce pathology. Religion, particularly the Judeo-Christian religion of divine grace, is a significant anxiety-reduction mechanism. Its unique theology of grace is that it reveals God as unconditionally gracious and universally forgiving, while many other religions, and the false Christianity conceived by many Christians, see God as a threat.

The anxiety-reducing factor in such false religions is legalistic self-righteousness and self-justification. That is a strategy of forcing God's favor toward us through the performance of liturgical or ethical requirements, devised by religionists, for measuring up to God's supposed standards or requirements. In authentic Christianity the anxiety-reduction mechanism is exclusively that of grace, "unconditional positive regard" for the person who has fallen short of God's way and will, namely, all of us. The anxiety reduction is reinforced, of course, by the opportunity of the life of gratitude that can follow so great a salvation, such fun and relief in being a believer (Rom 15:13). So the biblical theology of alienation is crucial to the Christian professional's perception of self and the other, and the recognition of God's way of dealing with that, as the Christian's analogue for handling people.

The *biblical theology of grace*, therefore, is critically informative of any sound psychological or psychotherapeutic concept or strategy (Ellens 2007). In the Bible grace is unconditional, arbitrary, universal, exploitable, and radical. It is unconditional as in the parable of the prodigal son, universal as in Genesis 12 and 17 covenant promise for the healing of all nations, and it is radical in that it cuts through all of our defenses and self-justifications to the center of human alienation, whether we like it or not, and resolves our problem at that level. Moreover, God's grace perpetually reaffirms the compatriot status of all humans with God, in spite of themselves.

That has been a difficult perception for the believing community to hold onto throughout history. The Jews took about 1000 years to lose their grip on it. Jesus cut back through to that core truth and it took the Christians about 500 years to completely lose their hold on it. Luther restored the insights of radical grace as the driving force of the Reformation. It took the Lutherans and Calvinists about 250 years to return to their scholasticism and discard unconditional grace. We are increasing the efficiency of our return to our native underlying proclivity to what is really pagan religion. Humans have a compulsive need to try to get our hands back on the controls of self-justification. Accepting free grace and simply trusting God for it is so scary and so nearly unbelievable for people who perceive themselves as "not OK children," or borderline syndrome psychotics who "know" that they are absolutely righteous and the whole world is wrong. The Christian model of pathology and patient care needs to be formed and informed by the radical realities of this biblical theology of grace.

The *biblical theology of sin* is likewise crucial to the perspectival model of the Christian psychotherapist. Sin, contrary to popular opinion, is a failure in achievement of authenticity of self and of full-orbed personhood as God designed us to be, it is a distraction to lesser achievements. It cannot be compensated for and it can only be converted from. *Metanoia* is the only solution. That is the biblical word for changing one's mind, choosing a new course or posture toward God and others. That is possible only to the person who has heard the announcement that he or she is forgiven and accepted unconditionally by God or another person.

Nietzsche averred that the courage to be, in this tragic world, is the ability to stand at the brink of the abyss of death and hear, without flinching, the announcement that God is dead. The real story is that the only courage for time and eternity, in this sick, fractured, and alienated world, is the ability to stand in the middle of the helplessness and hopelessness of human spiritual and emotional sickness and hear the announcement that God has embraced all of us, in spite of ourselves. That insight affords the realization that if God is for us no one and nothing can be against us.

Ultimately, each person cannot even be against himself or herself as an obstruction to divine grace, forgiveness, and acceptance. Such healing perception comes from really hearing the word that human destiny is to realize in full-orbed personhood the palpable experiences of the status of compatriot of God, which God has imputed to every human, in spite of ourselves. God never abrogates that human status. God simply waits for us to achieve the self-actualization that expresses it. Sin is falling short of that divine expectation and human longing. Sin is not the moralizing we make of it so we can fashion a self-justification by rationalizations, behavior changes, or bribes of God.

As Paul makes clear in his epistles, God's law is not a threat, implying that we have a conditional relationship with God, infractions bringing loss of favor. The law is an ancient Hebrew artifact and a constitution for a wholesome way of social and spiritual life. It is a guide to peace and prosperity. It is interesting that Jesus, and most of the prophets, were preoccupied with social and psychological wholeness, not with practices of private piety and personal purity. Such preoccupation is idolatry, manufacturing out of self a plastic doll, as opposed to celebrating the compatriot status that grace establishes. Sin is bondage and pathology, because it is a distraction to a distorted destiny, a constrained striving, compared with maturity in God's grace: the glorious freedom of the children of God (Ellens 2008).

Thus Luther could say, "Sin boldly," and mean it. "Since you are going to be a sinner today, step out boldly into today, living in the assurance of God's grace!"

The *biblical theology of discipline* is the theme of discipleship. Getting well or doing good is enacting grace. Discipline is the endeavor of beginning down the road of forgiveness of self and others, of acceptance of self and others, of unconditionally caring for self and others, and of reflecting the divine analogue. Discipleship is a troth with God to incarnate that divine grace-dynamic that infuses the universe. It is a troth "to forsake all other foci and to keep thee only to the God-designed destiny of growth in grace and graciousness."

Jesus urged people to such discipline by the grace he demonstrated in the way he handled them. The adulterous woman in John 8 he urged, "I do not condemn you. Go your way and do not do it anymore. It is not true to yourself." To the Samaritan woman in John 4 Jesus gave the insight that spirituality, not religiosity, is the issue. Peter, the denier, Jesus ordained to build the church. Matthew reports that when Jesus encountered Judas in the Garden he grabbed him and said, "Friend, how did it come to this?"

Biblical discipleship means being committed to God, to be free in grace. It means to live each moment as it were in God's favor and before God's smiling face. Since that is what life is designed to be, Christian expectations for therapists and Christian possibilities for clients will be shaped by such discipleship.

Henri Nouwen (1990) expressed the finest word on the *biblical theological theme of the wounded healer*. He took the suffering servant notion of Isaiah 53, which is also epitomized in the messianic theology of the New Testament, and pointed out that there are four doors for God and Christian therapists (healers), into the heart of humanity. First, there is the door of the woundedness of the world. Second, the woundedness of each generation. Third, the woundedness of persons. Fourth, the woundedness of the healer. He pointed out that the wounded healer theme implies that all grace, growth, and healing are communicated or incited by starting where the healer and the person to be healed are located on the continuum of life and growth. The humanness and brokenness of both must be affirmed. The healer's role is not to remove the pain of life but to interpret it. Moreover, the evidence in the healer of woundedness and pain, and of the transcendence or constructive endurance of all that, helps to heal the patient. Carl Jung's notion of the archetype healer projected by the patient upon the therapist, and the value of the healer sharing his or her own growth dynamics in therapy, are relevant here. The wounded healer can become the model and the incarnation of risk taking for growth and healing. The therapist's life and person can be the model that gives reason for the patient to have hope.

The *biblical theological theme of mortality* is directly related to the idea of the wounded healer. The Bible gives little impetus to the perfectionist notion that being God's person will eliminate the mortality and brokenness in the world. Instead it affirms our mortality and the world's brokenness, and emphasizes the strategies for making godly sense in that setting. That, after all, is what grace is all about. The brokenness, humanness, and pathology is affirmed—and that we are dying men and women in a generation of dying men and women.

This biblical theological theme of mortality acknowledges both the magnificence and malignancy in the universe. The persistent malignancy is pathologically denied in our cultural idealization of the bigger and better. The Bible says it is OK to vary from the idealized norm. It is acceptable to age, wrinkle, decrease, weaken, become more dependent, and even die. In fact, to die can be a real gain, according to Paul. Youthfulness is not the focus of meaning in the biblical concept of mortality, but maturation is. Patients need to feel in therapists the Christian realization that it is a supportable, and perhaps even a celebratable condition to be a human, mortal, dying person, before the face of God.

The finest biblical illumination of what it means behaviorally to be Christian in our work and world is the *biblical theological theme of celebration*. It is a revealing clinical and biblical fact, an empirical psychological and spiritual fact, that people who can be grateful can be healthy; and people who are incapable of generating spontaneous and authentic gratitude are unable to be healthy. They do not have the interior machinery or dynamics for it.

The German Reformers knew that to be true four hundred years ago and wrote it into the Heidelberg Catechism, with its focus upon gratitude as the Christian way of life. Celebration as gratitude may take the form of worship or a devoted posture toward God. Celebration may be exhilarated joy for the providence of God in life, or for the beauty of God's created world. To be Christian means to live in celebration of our Father's beneficence. A Christian therapist who sees life as that kind of enterprise will incarnate for the patient some crucial elements of celebration, in the spirit and tone of the clinical process.

Spirituality, Religion, and Science

TWELVE PRACTICAL APPLICATIONS

The twelve practical applications of biblical theology to the psychotherapeutic process can be detailed briefly.

1. Recognition of the biblical themes leads to the assumption of a pre-established identity for the patient. It is the identity of one whom God affirms as God's compatriot. That identity needs to be recovered or enhanced in the therapy. Though that may never be explained in the therapy, it will shape the therapist's affirmation of the patient and hence the patient's experience of being affirmed by the therapist. The therapist is in that sense a priest of God for that needy person.

2. The biblical themes imply for the patient a certified and secure destiny, infused with clear purpose for the patient's self-realization as a person who is working out his or her destiny in God's world.

3. This insures for the patient the experience of acceptance in keeping with the analogue of God's unconditional grace for the patient and the therapist. The biblical themes introduce into the therapeutic milieu a dynamic that can work toward the defusing of neurotic guilt, unproductive remorse, hopelessness, unresolved grief, self pity, compulsivity, and some of the need for schizoid ideation. That Christian perspective also potentially decreases the need for the self-defeating processes of masking, denial, self-justification, self-affliction, and the conversion reactions or reaction formation that are so often produced by these pathologies. Moreover, the insight afforded by the biblical themes frees one for informed and constructive self-acceptance.

4. The perspective that these themes give the therapist, and potentially the patient, provide the foundation for a life-style of dignity—not a life-style of self-abnegation and demeanment, but of being cherished and affirmed.

5. The biblical perspective can take the anxiety out of doing therapy, for the therapist. Since God is God and grace is grace, even when we are not experiencing it, the therapist need not feel as though the weight of the world is on him or her, and as though the therapist's own personhood or destiny hangs on the outcome of "this case."

6. These themes afford the relief, affirmed self-esteem, and certification that are likely to take the form of perceived inherent worthiness on

the part of the patient as person, rather that a sense of worthiness earned and dependent upon the patient's behavior or rate of healing, or capacity to please the therapist.

7. The biblical perspectives can decrease the amount of therapist-pathology with which the patient has to deal.
8. They provide a broad base of insight and perspective for building wholesome transference and countertransference.
9. These themes afford a coherent context for all of life, healthy or pathological. That context is God's disposition of inviolable goodwill, not divine threat.
10. They expand the potential for risk taking toward growth and integrated maturity, by means of their predominant function of constructive anxiety-reduction. The entire mode of these themes is freedom. They afford relief from constraints that distract from the patient's Christian self-actualization.
11. The biblical perspective frees the therapist to be human without being care-less; to play God as necessary in therapeutic decision-making and method without losing sight of his or her real stature and role; and to exercise a sound sense of humor about himself or herself, about God, about the patient and the therapist's and patient's pathology, and about the fragile enterprise of therapy.
12. The biblical perspectives release persons to die well. That relief attacks the ultimate panic that stands as a specter behind all pathology.

CONCLUSION

Spirituality and faith are cognitive-emotive processes. Therefore, their function for good or ill must be most relevant and applicable to disorders that are cognitive or emotive in source. That means that healthy dynamics and perspectives in theology and faith will affect the potential health of the therapist and patient in such psychosocial disorders. Religious dynamics may be somewhat less relevant in psychopathology that has a body-chemistry source, though even there, healthy theology and wholesome faith may be invaluable in management of the symptoms.

There is increasing evidence for the two-way switching function of the hypothalamus in channeling or controlling the impact of the endocrine disorders upon the psychological field, and of psychic disorders upon the endocrine function. This suggests that the role of healthy or pathological theology, religion, or spirituality becomes increasingly interesting with regard to the role in even those psychopathologies that appear to be rooted in distortions of body chemistry.

Therefore, concerns about theological and spiritual perspectives, faith commitments, religious experience, and spiritual maturity are becoming increasingly vital therapeutic issues. The concern to be an effective Christian professional really is a crucial one. The following chapters endeavor to explore the issues raised in this chapter.

3

The Interface of Psychology and Theology

THE BIBLICAL STORY, AS a paradigm of the human psychological and spiritual odyssey, asserts an inherent union of our experience of history and God's. In the picture that the Bible paints, this is God's world and we live in it. The import of that centers in the reality that life for God, as Spirit, and the life of the human psyche interact, interface, or cut across each other at such a substantive or foundational level as to affect the description and definition of both our psyches and God as Spirit. To employ a meaningful and authentic theology (concept of God) requires a useful and honest anthropology (concept of humankind). To engage anthropology thoroughly and exhaustively lands one finally in theology. One must come at each with an eye to the other. The same can be said as well about the science of any other facet of the cosmos, God's created world.

So religion is barren without a comprehensive appreciation of creation, and creation at the center can only be comprehensively understood religiously. The natural and social sciences must inquire finally of theology. Theology must listen and speak to the natural and social sciences. Psychology is an applied social science with a base in the natural sciences, just as medicine, education, and preaching. Psychology properly exercises the stewardship of its mandate by collecting data, formulating theories that account for the data, and applying the interpreted data to concerns in psychotherapy.

Theory development is a religious act. It hinges upon one's point of view and one's outlook on life, namely, it is an act with a faith assumption behind it. Theory development is one of the key intersections of the natural and social sciences with theology, in that it involves both the assessment of the natural or social science and the application of a world-view assumption to it. That intersection shapes and constrains everything in the natural and social sciences.

This chapter addresses some of the implications of a thoroughgoing grace theology for psychology theory development. It will emphasize the problem of the intersection of theology and psychology and the import of a Christian anthropology for responsible development of personality theory. Subsequent chapters will then consider the problem of a theology of illness, and the psychological theory of healing, wholeness, and redemption, and related clinical concerns.

THE INTERSECTION OF THEOLOGY AND PSYCHOLOGY

Egbert Schuurman was a professor of Christian philosophy at Eindhoven Institute of Technology and lecturer in the philosophy of culture at the Vrije Universität te Amsterdam. He wrote a book some years ago that might be considered a model for handling the issue of relationship between the claims of a Christian confessional worldview and the scientific enterprise. The book is titled *Technology and the Future: A Philosophical Challenge* (2009). Schuurman does not follow the pattern of those Christians who reject technology for society, or of those who look toward technology as the avenue of salvation for our culture. In his important volume he advocates for an integration of Christian belief and philosophical or scientific thought.

In a true integration like that, fresh light is allowed to fall on the problems that the positivist empiricists and the post-modernists raise, and upon the mutually contradictory solutions they propose. The one group is oriented to human freedom, the other to technological power. Freedom and power exist for them in an eternally unbridgeable dichotomy and must be harmonized in this fresh light.

Professionals concerned with the intersection of theology and psychology must, of course, follow a similar course in the present quest. After a profound analysis of both extremes of freedom and power, Schuurman develops the basis for the distinctive contributions the natural and social sciences—and technology—can make. In his previous book, *Reflections of the Technological Society* (1980), he presents an interplay between modern philosophy and modern technology. Christian psychologists must do the counterpart of that in our discipline.

Stanley L. Jaki, a distinguished Benedictine priest with doctorates in both systematic theology and physics, has taken a similar approach, somewhat closer to the problem of the relationship between psychology and theology. His *The Road of Science and the Ways to God* (1978) demonstrates from the history of science what a key role rational theology has had in the rise of science and its plethora of applied achievements. He confirms Francis Bacon's choice remark upon the obverse of the argument, namely, that a little philosophy (science) leads one to atheism, but profound philosophy (comprehensive and exhaustive) leads one to theism.

In *Cosmos and Creator* (1980), the Gifford Lectures, Jaki explored the connection between the anthropology that functions in the natural and social sciences, handled from a secular and Christian perspective. Jaki promises to illumine and enhance our quest to understand the interface of the psychological and theological sciences. His thrust, like Schuurman's, assumes the essential legitimacy of the secular scientific quest for truth, expects productivity from what the natural and social sciences can offer, and is optimistic about what the theological sciences may produce. He honors what each brings to their intersection with each other and from their dialogue. He considers that the crucial element will be the quality of the perspective each offers regarding the other, and regarding their own subject matter.

Except for the lunatic fringe of ultra-fundamentalists, there has been a constant and consistent urgency among Christians to avoid forcing a perceived dichotomy between faith and science, or forcing a contrived unity between the two. God does not speak with a forked tongue, so we must assume that what we learn in nature about God's story for us, and what we learn in scripture about God's story for us, are a unified revelation. God speaks in nature and in grace, in God's created world and in the world of the word of the Bible. The Christian professional is called to embody a sound theology and a sound psychology on the assumption that thus both will come out with sophisticated application and scientific integrity.

Our perspectival model of the interface of psychology and theology inspired us to look for the way each scientific enterprise, theology and psychology, may profit from the light that each can bring to the other's science. Each of these scientific endeavors may be approached from the perspective of the other and, hence, each may be formed and informed by the other. If both are thoroughly pursued there can be no tension between them in the long run. Each tells the story of the human person in its own way. Telling that same story from two different directions with two different symbol systems is not the same as saying two different things. What the Bible and science say, touching history and the cosmos do not stand in an inherent inconsistency.

It seems to me that there are four areas in which the sciences of psychology and theology interact: at the work of Theory Development Level, at the design of Research Methodology, at the mode of collection of the Data Base Level, and at the Clinical Function Level. These are the places of intersection at which constructive work can be done in relating our faith to our professions and the science of psychology to the science of theology. At these junctures or nodes each must illumine the other or both are deprived of the comprehensiveness of a robust and honest science.

Figure 7

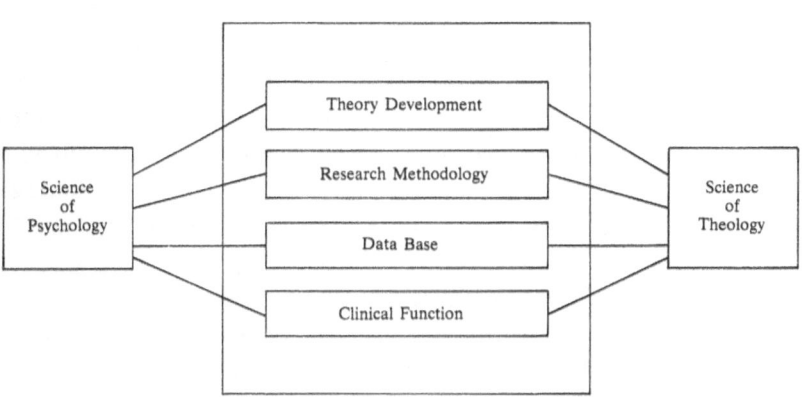

Moreover, these four levels of scientific inquiry always remain interactive, mutually forming and informing the shape and perspective of each of the other levels. Then we can be integrated persons, who are sophisticated Christian believers and sophisticated psychologists. At the level of personal function, I think, is the location where the term *integration* is relevant. A correct perspectival model of theology and psychology can produce integrated Christian professional persons.

Figure 8

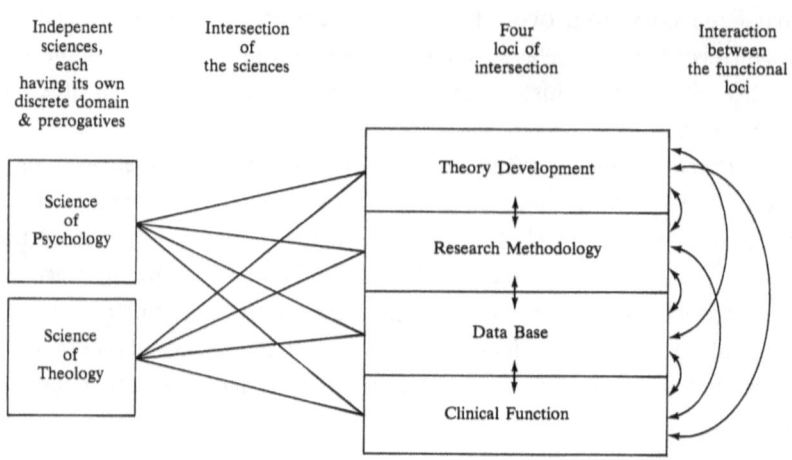

It may be urged that instead of thinking of a tension, let us assume an integral and inherent harmony between our faith and feelings, between the scientific products of our theology and our psychology, between our scientific view of persons and our experiences of them. Human nature is a unity, centered in a creature who is psychical and physical, but yet spiritual at the core. We need not construct a unity between psychology and theology but merely to discover the integral unity there, allowing the phenomena to reveal to us their authentic integrity.

We have noted that theology and psychology intersect at the levels of *theoretical assumptions, research methodology, database management, and clinical application.* They are busy forming and informing one another at each level. The subject of study at each level is the human person. It is apparent, therefore, that the phenomenon in which the intersections of theology and psychology are discerned and realized is the *anthropological model* that functions or is forming at each of the four levels of intersection.

One might say that an engine runs on gasoline in gaseous form and on oxygen and hydrogen molecules in gaseous form. One might further explain that the engine works because in it these two gaseous elements, gasoline and air, intersect, forming and informing each other. For an especially interested student, one might go on to explain that the intersection is evident at various levels, at the level of the carburetor and at the level of combustion chamber in the cylinder. With an even more precocious student one might continue and suggest that the specific component in which the intersecting gas and air interact is the Venturi tube in the carburetor. In autos these days, of course, you would need to mention the fuel injectors instead of carburetors.

I see something like that as the role of the anthropological component in each of the loci of intersection of theology and psychology. *That* concept of the nature of humanness is functioning or forming there that each of the sciences brings to the intersection, and both are mutually illumining and shaping the intersection. The integrality of the whole is realized then, in terms of the anthropological authenticity we experience regarding the impact of psychology and theology in our assumptions and theory development; our research methodology and hypotheses; our data collection sources, methods, and designs; and our clinical function and fruitfulness. The authenticity of that process will manifest itself in the theoretical formulation and in the empirical experience of the outcome.

Figure 9

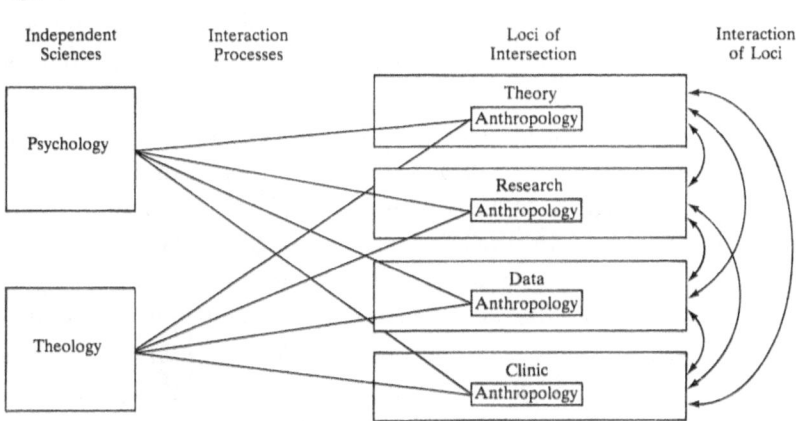

The anthropological concept that is forming or funtioning in each locus of intersection is the actual junction element that constitutes the cite of intersection.

So, sound pursuit of the inevitably religious enterprise of psychology theory development, informed by our best insights from speculation, research, empirical evidence, and clinical experience, will inevitably be a conscious and creative quest for a warrantable *anthropology*. If we can thus achieve a warrantable concept of the nature of humans, we will be able to formulate an authentic personality theory, theories of pathology, and theories of healing, wholeness, and wholesomeness.

The key problem for developing a warrantable anthropology within the ferment of the intersection of theology and psychology is one of establishing the criteria for judging truth as truth, and apparent truth as falsehood. This book is not going to solve that problem but, rather, focus it and hold out for two critical elements in that solution. Further study will be necessary at precisely this location if the dialogue regarding science and the Christian faith is to move ahead. We, as the community of Christian psychologists, have danced all around this issue but have not resolved the impasse. We must do that or our digestion of the relationship of theology and psychology will again be as constipated and fruitless as it was three or four decades ago.

Let us push the matter forward with the following observations. First, the scientific method, classically formulated by Aristotle, Aquinas, and Francis Bacon, is indispensable to our investigation of both the psychological and theological sciences if we are to obey the first principle of Christian scientific theory development, namely, that our theories must be warrantable and certifiable theories. Warrantable means that they are as thoroughly in conformity to the whole truth at our disposal as we have the resources to make possible.

The second critical element in the solution of the problem of norms and criteria for adjudging truth is awareness that truth to the Greeks (*alytheia*) was one thing, and to the Hebrew Bible tradition (*'emeth*) it was quite another. The modern world of science and technology has been uniformly dominated by the Greek notion of truth, with its implied rational empiricism. Post modernism has called that notion into question with very good reason. As scientists now acknowledge, there is a wide world of truth to be known outside the boundaries of what can be accessible through rational empirical means. This is a mindset or realization that seems to long for the Hebrew model of truth.

Thorlief Boman, in *Hebrew Thought Compared with Greek* (1960), argued that for the Greek, truth was that which is evident, clear, and seen. For the Hebrew Bible, truth is that which is dependable, faithful, and trustworthy. The Greek notion deals with objectivity, the Hebrew with subjectivity. Hebrew truth is not metaphysical, but characterological, phenomenological, heuristic, and covenantal or interpersonal. It is, for example, a matter of trust between persons, including God and humans.

It is not surprising that in the worldview of the biblical theologian, as long ago as the earliest pages of holy scripture, the idea that God had covenanted with humanity to guarantee certain basic truths, such as God's universal forgiving grace: forgiveness for everybody, for everything, for evermore (Genesis 12 and 17). This upholds the human status of God-compatriot, a status never to be abrogated under any circumstance. Neither is it surprising that the Hebrew tradition was not recorded in philosophical treatises like those of the classical Greek humanists. It was preserved instead, in the very personal record of human experience of, and perceptions about, the mighty acts of God in human history. For the Greeks, truth was evidential and hence static through time, inherent in creation, as are mathematical facts. For the Hebrews truth was dynamic, unfolding through time, implied in creation but realized in the perpetual process of the redemptive and providential process of recreation, unveiling, and revelation in human experience.

Greek truth required one to stand outside the system and observe the evidence and logic of it. Hebrew truth required one to stand inside the system to feel and hear the confirmation of the dynamic process of truth exuding from experience, unveiling, a process of discovery. Even the word of the prophets and of the man from Nazareth, the incarnate Logos, was ultimately useful to the degree that it became a personal encounter with a truth from God.

To establish adequate criteria for assessing the data of experience, or of rational reflection, or of logical deduction, as truth, it is imperative that we devise sound strategy and tactics for applying the constraints of the scientific method to the Hebrew type of truth. Abraham Maslow's insistence upon the truth-value of the world of feelings and emotions (1992) has radically revised our culture's perception of truth and moved us solidly into the post-modern way of thinking. This orientation has been greatly advanced by the work of Positive Psychology, especially that of Marty Seligman (*Flourish*, 2012; *Authentic Happiness*, 2002).

This post-modern way of thinking argues that all truth is not "out there" and objective; to be seen best from the outside in, observed from the point of view of a spectator. Post-Modernism has compelled us to deal with the reality that there is a vast world of phenomenological truth which is relatively subjective and is best appreciated from the inside out, that is, from within the experience as it is happening. Client-centered therapy is built largely upon this hypothesis, devolving from a specific anthropological view that very much crucial truth, especially that which is relevant in the clinical setting, is psychological and personal in the Hebraic sense.

It is clearly the case that both of these perspectives on truth are correct regarding those arenas of truth to which each applies. They are scientifically useful when held together. It is intriguing to notice that Aristotle, the father of the scientific method, in his move away from Platonic speculative idealism to rational empiricism, was aware of this crucial insight. He preferred to think of himself, not as a philosopher in the Pythagorean tradition, but as a psychologist. However, he never worked out this issue or moved beyond the classical view of truth. It is likely that if Western ecclesiastical development had followed Aurelius Augustine, however, as the Eastern Church did, instead of Anselm and Aquinas and the unresolved problem of Aristotelianism, the modern era would have been shaped by a Hebrew notion of truth and method, rather than Greek. That posture of truth as subjective and covenantal, rather than objective and empirical, is still evident in the Eastern Church's preference for theology as celebration. This is a psychological phenomenon, versus the Western Church's preference for theology that is propositional and nomistic, an essentially logic phenomenon.[1]

The force of contemporary psychology and the oriental notions of truth impinging upon the West from Eastern Religions are moving American culture toward a balance between Greek and Hebrew perceptions of truth. That will make us more able to employ sound anthropology and help resolve the quest for the Christian interface of theology and psychology.

PSYCHOLOGICAL ANTHROPOLOGY

While theological anthropology tends to follow either a biblical theological concept of the nature of human beings or the philosophical theological perspective of Paul Tillich, psychological anthropology takes the form of a variety of personality theories. One of the most helpful is that of Salvadore R. Maddi (1996). Maddi's study treats the classic theorists from Freud to Seligman in terms of two primary categories: the manner in which each theory illumines matters regarding the core of human personality and the way each treats the periphery of human personality. Within these two categories he describes each theory in terms of its essence as a conflict model or a fulfillment model of personality. He presents his own model, which he calls the consistency model, and then critiques each in terms of rational

---

1. It would be interesting at this juncture to explore the relative role of right brain dominance and left brain dominance of the Eastern and Western Churches' approaches and of the Augustinian and Aristotelian approaches, respectively; see Restak (1988).

empirical criteria, applicable to both of the primary categories of core and periphery. Maddi defines personality as

> a stable set of characteristics and tendencies that determine those commonalities and differences in the psychological behavior (thoughts, feelings, and actions) of people that have continuity in time and that may not be easily understood as the sole result of social and biological pressures of the moment. Tendencies are the processes that determine directionality of thought, feelings, and actions. They are in the service of goals or functions. Characteristics are static or structural entities, usually implied by tendencies, that are used to explain not the movement toward goals or the achievement of function but rather the fact and content of goals or requirements (Maddi, 10).

So human personality is a concept used to describe the observed phenomena that indicate the kind of person a given individual is, as indicated by his or her type of response to life situations. The interpretation, of course, implies a perspective determined by one's essential assumptions regarding the nature of humanness. The anthropology operating is that concept of human nature that is functioning or forming in the interplay of those assumptions and the observed phenomena (data).

Core attributes of personality are those features that disclose the inherent attributes of humans. Periphery facets of personality, according to Maddi, are learned not inherent. They are concrete and close to the behavior itself, which is observed. Concerning the conflict, fulfillment, and consistency models, Maddi makes the follow points.

The conflict model assumes that personality is the product of two great opposing and unchangeable forces, functioning at the psychosocial or the intra-psychic level, between which forces the person is achieving a dynamic balance, or a denial of either or both. The fulfillment model assumes only one force, localized in the person, and moving toward either actualization or perfection. The consistency model assumes no great dynamic forces at all, but rather a dynamic growth process of interaction with and feedback from the environment. "(I)f the feedback is consistent with what is expected, or with what has been customary, there is quiescence. But if there is inconsistency between the feedback and the expectation or custom, there is pressure to decrease this uncomfortable state of affairs. Life is understood as the extended attempt to maintain consistence" (Maddi, 24).

Maddi cites Freud and Murray as representing the conflict model, psychosocial version; Rank, Jung, Perls, and others as examples of the conflict model, intra-psychic version. Rogers, Maslow, and Seligman illustrate the fulfillment model actualization version; Adler, White, Allport, Fromm, and Ellis, the fulfillment model, perfection version. The consistency model, cognitive dissonance version includes the work of Kelly, McClelland, and Festinger; the consistency model, activation version, that of Fiske and Maddi.

It is precisely within the personality theory prevailing in each anthropological concept that is forming or functioning within each locus that the sciences of psychology and theology intersect. The critical issue here is the need to ferret out the anthropological assumptions and consequences of each of these personality theories and to determine how, in the interplay between the assumptions and the data, the psycho-theological anthropology is being shaped. This is crucial for determining how one may responsibly bring a grace theology—formulated as the principles and perspectives of a tentative biblical anthropology—to bear on the interpretation of the observed behavioral data. Does it foster a soundly mature theological and psychological anthropology and personality theory?

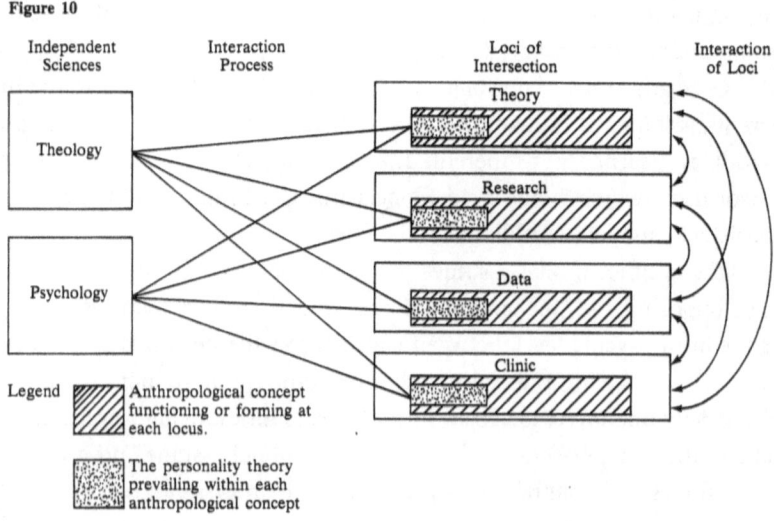

Figure 10

CONCLUSION

What must be asserted first, in drawing conclusions from all this, is that neither the biblical assumptions nor the empirical or psychological data has a higher warrant as truth or a higher logical, psychological, or theological valence than the other. Both must vitally participate in the interface of assumptions and data, for a mature anthropology and personality theory to evolve.

Secondly, it is the contention of this chapter that the assumptions of the God-compatriot model of human status and the God-imager model of human nature, cast in terms of the evident brokenness of humans, are a crucial part of the assessment that must be fed into the personality theory model. Moreover, this entire set of phenomena must be formulated in terms of the reality of the radical, unconditional and uncalculating, and universal nature of God's covenant grace. This is an absolutely crucial assumption to bring to bear upon the data, with a view to achieving an authentic psycho-theological theory-development process. Not only is this true in the area of personality theory development, but in all other areas of psychology theory development as well.

Third, a sound theory must be operational, in the sense that it provides adequate tools for the handling of concept definition and the associated concept measurement necessary to manage authentically the full range of data. A sound theory also must be precise, in that it must deal with the data pertinent to the specified problem or concern. Furthermore, it must be empirically, philosophically, and psychologically valid, in the sense that it manages the full range of data from all sources: empirical data, philosophical theological assumptions, and psychological perceptions.

Fourth, psycho-theology theory development is crucial at each level of the intersection of psychology and theology: conceptual theory, research methodology, database management, and clinical experience.

Fifth, there is a wide variety of personality theories, as Maddi sees them, or as in the Hall-Lindsey (1978) categories: psychoanalytic, psychological, personological, field theory, individual, oranismic, factor theory, S-R, operant-reinforcement, self psychology, existential, and behaviorist. They all really come down to four types: rational, emotional, relational, and biological theories. For example, one might place Ellis in the First, Maslow and Rogers in the second, Perls and Erhard in the third, and Skinner in the fourth.

If one assumes humans to be essentially rational, that affects one's theory of education and healing (therapy), because it affects one's psycho-theology of immaturity and illness. It suggests that illness is a deficit of appropriate information or coherence, as is immaturity. Education and healing require information and insight. If one assumes humans to be essentially emotional in nature, education and healing require sensitivity and freedom; immaturity and illness are from blocked emotionality. Relationality as a model of how persons are, assumes the need for confrontation and interaction as states in which persons realize their actualized personhood. The biological definition of human nature assumes that illness or immaturity is the result of inappropriate stimuli, producing a pathological state of response. So both healing and education require the introduction of a proper S-R process.

When one applies such categories as these to our work, the crucial role one's anthropology plays in one's psychology theory development is readily evident. One can see how real the essentially religious nature of scientific theory development is. How crucial a difference is made in sound psychology theory development by the enrollment of a biblical anthropology into the interaction of theological assumptions and data and psychological assumptions and data!

Sixth, at the very least, sound biblical anthropology will disclose the fact that each of the four types of personality theory indicated above contains theologically valid elements: rational, emotional, relational, and biological. A full-fledged Christian theory requires adequate comprehension of all these elements. Likewise, though a biblical theology seems to me to militate in favor of Maddi's fulfillment model, actualization version, with such representatives as Rogers, Maslow, Seligman, and the Positive Psychologists, it must be said that, were one to adopt Maddi's categories completely, a sound biblical anthropology would disclose crucial truth in each of the models listed.

Seventh, if a sound psycho-theological anthropology is crucial to personality theory development, it will be crucial, as well to the development of a theory of illness, a theory of wholeness, and a theory of healing (therapy).

In sum, I see theology and psychology as different perspectives or frames of reference, with differing terminology, dealing with the same subject matter. Allport emphasized the importance of translating insights and concepts from each science for the other. They interact at four levels in the quest for truth about their subject: at the theoretical level of assumptions and concept and theory definition, at the research methodology level, at the data base level (what data to look for, how, management of the data), and clinical experience level. Their common subject is humanness or the nature of human beings. They intersect, therefore, in the anthropology that is functioning or forming at each level of intersection. The function and formation of anthropology at each level must continually form and inform the anthropology that is forming and functioning at all the other levels. Thus may the total range of potential insight in this quest for the truth about psychology and theology totally form and inform each other. Thus the entire enterprise will operate in terms of an authentic and unified personality theory. That makes possible a Christian enterprise in the helping professions.

4

Anxiety and the Rise of Religious Experience

HUMAN RELIGION IS UNIVERSAL. Religious experience and expression is evidenced by and significantly shapes all culture. Apparently to be religious is native to being human.

People everywhere worship. To do so seems innate in human personality. Liturgies of worship grow out of psychological and spiritual sources deep within human personality. Those psychic sources of religion are closely related to the native anxiety patterns discernible in persons. Some forms of worship and religion meet the deep human psychic needs better than other forms. Most religious practices in life and history reinforce the anxiety of humans through the frustrating dynamics of guilt and shame, and the sense of our ultimate helplessness in the face of the problems of morality and mortality. Authentic Judeo-Christianity is unique in its gospel of grace. That cuts to the center of the problem with the assurance of both the meaningfulness of life and the promise of immortality. Distinguishing between what is authentic spirituality and what is psychic pathology is therefore, crucial.

Already in the antique world of Greece and Rome, it was strongly suggested that all humans need to worship. Despite the Renaissance, a sixteenth-century movement toward secular humanism, modern thought has consistently suspected that the ancient suggestion of the universality of the human need to worship is accurate. Since Sir James George Frazer's notable work, *The Golden Bough* (2002), was first published in 1890 the Western world has scientifically affirmed that humanness and religiosity always and everywhere appear together. The Eastern world has known the certainty of that fact for a number of millennia.

The only remaining potential challenge to this axiom about religion and humanness lies with the paleontologists, like the Leakey family, who presume to uncover the character and culture of the original hominids and hominoids. They have gained great ground in their endeavors. They may turn up a pre-religious hominid. However, the current evidence is against it, since among the earliest tools of all anthropoids so far identified, ritual and funerary instruments and objects of an apparently religious nature have been included. If some anthropologist looks one day into the sunken sockets of a pre-religious hominid skull, of course, there will still remain the problem of definition of terms. How will we certify that the primitive character who lost his apparently godless head so long ago was really pre-religious in theological tendencies as well as in his tools? How, moreover, will it be decided which hominoid was hominid and which hominid was Homo Sapiens?

Humanness as we know it, in any case, is apparently essentially religious. Scholars in the field of comparative religion have unveiled a wealth of information in the last hundred and fifty years concerning the nature and meaning of the religious character of humanness. In so doing, they have demonstrated the significant religious role of symbol in theology and ritual. Out of recognition of the universal religious role of symbols and symbol-making arose the awareness of intricate interrelationship between religion and human psychology—between the life of the spirit and the life of the psyche (Jung 1964).

In the last half century vigorous and productive work has been done in the psychology of religion. The enterprise has depended heavily upon the pioneering work of William James (1911, 2009) and his *Varieties of Religious Experience*. That in turn was anticipated in theology by the epistemological quest of Immanuel Kant and by the entire fabric of the theology of Schleiermacher. It was Schleiermacher, after all, who defined the common ground from which all religious experiences grow. He built his Christian theology upon the fact that the feeling of dependence is the universal and constant character of human consciousness that makes humans necessarily religious. Carl Jung (1958) produced a major step forward in relating the world of the spirit and the world of the psyche with his description of human anxiety as the form in which we realize the experience of dependence. Seward Hiltner (1963) carried the idea from anxiety to the relief of grace.

Human religious experience and expression, it is therefore urged, rises from the native and universal human experience of anxiety. Arapura (1973), in his superb little book, *Religion as Anxiety and Tranquility*, refers to the non-accidental but necessary character of religion (7). He illumines the matter greatly by pointing out that the essential or necessary character of human religiosity is a product of human self-consciousness, which like *being* is what *necessarily is*. He goes on to argue that as humanness implies self-consciousness, it in turn implies anxiety, and anxiety is in interplay with the vital urges of the human organism toward achieving tranquility.

Karen Horney (1994) illumines this point with her useful definition of anxiety. After describing the kinship of anxiety with fear, she goes on to point out that when a mother fears her child will die because there is a pimple on the child's arm or a slight rash, we speak of her reaction as anxiety. If she is worried when her child has something serious, we call her discomfort fear. When someone fears to stand on a high bridge or deliver a speech he knows very well, it is anxiety. If he is afraid he will lose his way when he is in unfamiliar terrain in a bad storm he feels fear. If he fears driving his car across any bridges, he has anxiety. Fear is proportional to the danger. Anxiety is a disproportionate reaction to a threatening situation, one causing discomfort, or an imagined threat. The distinction is simple but of great importance.

Horney's point here is similar to Freud's distinction between objective and neurotic anxiety. Freud called the former a reasonable reaction to danger and the latter an irrational or exaggerated one. Horney is dissatisfied, however, to allow her simple definition to stand untouched. It has one flaw in her judgment. It does not distinguish between what is proportionate in one culture from what is disproportionate in another. Anxiety about taboos may be appropriate in the value setting of a primitive culture. Anxiety about the same thing in twenty-first-century American culture would be disproportionate and neurotic.

So she suggests a change in the definition. Fear and anxiety are both proportionate reactions to danger, but in the case of the former the danger is transparent and objective but in the case of anxiety it is not so overtly obvious and may be hidden or subjective. That is, the intensity of the anxiety is appropriate to the person's sense of the meaning the situation has for him or her but the reason why it makes such a person anxious is not clear to that person. This means that trying to persuade a neurotic to give up the anxiety is useless. The problem is not the reality he or she faces but a situation that appears to that person to be dangerous. That is the difference between fear and anxiety.

The perception to which Horney refers at this juncture is often a subconscious perception of an anxiety-affording situation. Humans often have anxiety, therefore, without being clearly aware of it. Nonetheless, that anxiety calls for resolution. The native forces of the human physical and psychic organism that press for tranquility function as vigorously on the subconscious as on the conscious level. People will find many ways to escape the sources of anxiety or to stop feeling it.

The fact that anxiety, whether disproportionate or proportionate, conscious or subconscious, is frequently irrational and manifests itself in irrational pressures toward resolution, does not discount the problem but rather complicates it. Irrational anxiety or expression of anxiety stimulates an admonition that something within us is out of gear and, therefore, it is a challenge to modify something in our inner world. The human organism employs four strategies to effect that change. Humans rationalize, deny, or narcotize anxiety, or repress thoughts, feelings, impulses, and experiences that might give rise to it. In the character and potential creativity of these forms of anxiety management lies the human religious potential.

Albert C. Outler (1997) assessed this precisely and positively. He said that religious anxiety is both neurotic and reality oriented at the same time. It is inappropriate if it is a reaction to a misunderstanding of our ontological groundlessness. This produces a kaleidoscope of religious superstitions and distortions of reality. Our perception of our alienation from God is turned around into a sense that God is alienated from us. God is a dreadful threat to the soul that misconstrues the nature of guilt and grace. This produces anxiety. Augustine called this a suspension over an abyss. He had anxiety about the ocean which reminded him of the unsteadiness and insecurity of life. This sense of disequilibrium arouses the feeling of life's greatest threat—life without meaning!

That inner dread of the ground of our being disappearing from under our feet is anxiety. However, the truth is the firmness of our footing, regardless of our character or behavior, in the certitude of the grace of the one who created and sustains the world. God's nature and character is our Ground and our End. Out of this ferment between anxiety and tranquility is awakened human spirituality and are generated human religious experiences and expression. Religion is part of the machinery for mediation between the forces of death and meaninglessness, on the one hand, and the security of life in grace, on the other.

How and why anxiety is aroused in humans and gives rise to religion is, of course, a further question. Another matter still, is the question of the efficiency with which religions of various kinds succeed in managing or responding to the native human angst. In observing the religious quest of the ancient Egyptians, Barbara Mertz (1966) signified the commonality of their predicament with ours and all humans four millennia later. She described the universal human need and genius for religion in her closing paragraph.

> Whether they feared their demons or not, the Egyptians did fear death—the first physical death and that second death from which there is no resurrection. They spent a good part of their lives fighting annihilation, and in so doing they built up the most complicated structure of mortuary ritual any people ever produced. We are the beneficiaries of it, in terms of museum collections and scholarly books; and perhaps we will not find the painted mummy cases and weird amulets so bizarre if we see beneath their extravagance, a common human terror and a common hope. (367)

That common human terror and common hope is the springboard of all religion. The Egyptian system may not have been as effective or as true as contemporary Christianity, but the crucial point here is that both spring from the same native humanness, and endeavor to meet the same need.

What then is that need? It seems apparent that all humans wrestle with four basic questions regarding the meaning of things. The questions concern origins, nature and destiny, the "oughts" of life, and aesthetics. To be human seems invariably to mean that we have a thirst to know where things come from, where things are going, what we ought, therefore, to do (ethics and moral code), and how we ought to carry ourselves (style). In addition the native human need to know what is the good, true, and beautiful makes everyone in some degree an aesthete, a seeker after beauty. All that is a function of human spirituality. I define spirituality as the universal, irrepressible, human hunger for meaning. That hunger for meaning involves all those aspects of the human quest.

All these major questions represent, and together comprehend, that massive world of the unknown into which the lately womb-harbored infant comes bumping and splashing down the birth canal. From the moment of birth, obviously, humans begin the long, psychologically arduous adventure of accommodation to the massive, mostly uncontrollable, and therefore threatening unknown of life in this world. Nearly as soon as the newly self-conscious child achieves some measure of control, stability, and security in his or her ever-expanding new world, he or she is imposed upon by a newer and even more unmanageable unknown: death.

All of us find that the arduous and threatening adventure is mostly, and ultimately, a tragic adventure. Born of this anxiety, then, is the perpetual human tension of mind and spirit between the paradise of tranquility we can envision and the possibilities of terror we really experience. The "once and future paradise" becomes a permanent part of our psychic symbolism and character. Obviously, for humans it is a relatively short step from such symbolics to the fashioning of God or gods "after our own image." We readily conclude, then, that this is the way things are.

The question should be raised, however, why humans need to deal so gravely and seriously with those four major meaning questions in life. Why is it not possible for humans, as Harry Golden (1960) counseled in his book, simply to relax and *Enjoy, Enjoy*? The answer, I judge, is the persistent presence of the problem of evil.

It is a fact of life that all of us begin, nearly as soon as we become self-conscious, to discern that we are all capable, at one and the same time, of being majestically magnificent and of being miserably malicious. We learn early, I believe, that there is in the universe itself a comparable potential for magnificence and malignancy. In the face of that and the anxiety it reinforces in us, we are driven to the pursuit of meaning. Likely there is something of the divine image in that insatiable quest.

It was this impasse regarding the incongruity of evil, finally, that shaped Søren Kierkegaard's definition of angst and religion. Rudolf Otto looked for the definitive stuff of religion in *das numinöse Gefühl*, a kind of mystical or intuitive level of self-consciousness in the presence of the human predicament, which would afford revelation of the certainty and character of God's existence. Mircea Eliade (1959) seems to be closer to the realities of experience and fact when he asserts that the human quest for meaning arises out of the "terror of history."

Eliade asks how we can possibly resolve the fact that we are caught between a psychospiritual rock and a hard place, so to speak. On the one hand we are irreparably stuck in *time*, irremediably caught in history. On the other hand, we know we will be damned, that is, we will find things ultimately meaningless if we allow ourselves to be lost in temporality and historicity, if our meaning does not transcend or reach beyond it. Therefore, we must of absolute necessity find, *in this temporal life*, an avenue to a transhistorical and atemporal plane. Our aspirations are inevitably a reach for the transcendent.

"Our common human terror," Eliade argues (1959), is our anxious awareness of the terminal character of finitude. Paul Tillich (1957) observed that finitude in awareness is anxiety. Our "common hope" is the paradise that comes with transcending finitude, which paradise we can envision but hardly create. To achieve meaning, namely, the certainty that historical tragedies have a transhistorical meaning, is to achieve freedom from finitude and anxiety, declares Eliade. That achievement is the business of religion, the behavior that expresses our spirituality.

Arapura summarizes the entire discussion when he suggests that we all are conscious at some level, of the wrongness or essential conflictedness of existence in this world. This sense of the disjointedness of life apparently surfaces especially in anxiety about our morality and our mortality. Religious experience and expression is the dynamic process of attempting to structure a response to the facts that we are dying, dealing with mortality, namely, the unknown of death; and we feel, therefore, inadequate in dealing with our morality, that is our potential loss of worthiness and worthwhileness. The religious dimension of humans is the psychological machinery and ritual tools produced by the human organism to manage that insecurity.

Religion, as spiritually induced behaviour, is a process for reducing the profound anxiety about the challenge of daily existence and the ultimate deadliness of life. It has the capacity to lift the meaning-hungry human spirit to the profound tranquility of salvation: eternal life as a quality of existence, now and ultimately. Spirituality is inherent in humans—the hunger for meaning. Religion is the behaviors, programs, documents, intellectual reflections, and rituals, by which we express that personal spirituality and act it out in order to reduce our anxiety about our finitude or the temporality of our existence.

In this anxiety reduction process it is a relatively short step from anxiety, the sense of wrongness internalized as personal guilt, to the projection upon the human universe of a concept of a threatening God. As children do, so do all humans, internalize threat and pain as guilt. If we are guilty, we are guilty before the face of someone who stands in a position of power and authority. So from the threat of the unknown within and without, humans move to anxiety, hence to guilt and a sense of the wrongness of things, and from guilt to a projection called a dangerous God.

The seriousness of this dynamic is not changed by Nietzsche's point that the bad conscience often produces much creative energy and productivity. Nietzsche said that a bad conscience is a sickness, but it is an illness like pregnancy is. The seriousness of the dynamic religious process, from anxiety, to guilt, to God, usually produces an ultimate psychological and theological impasse rather than a resolution of anxiety (Jung 1958). Taking the whole of the history of human religion into view, it is immediately apparent that normally what one compulsively is driven to undertake in religious quest one does not have the ability to achieve, namely, transcendence above finitude, morality, mortality, and the perceived divine threat.

Consequently, what humans usually achieve in their reach from anxiety, to guilt, to God is a god fashioned in our own threat image. That god then reigns as superego, imposing constraint not freedom, exaggerated anxiety not relief, legalistic rituals in worship and ethical and moral life and not the peace of God's forgiving grace. The only alternative in the history of religions has been the Judeo-Christian concept of grace: God who arbitrarily transcends the "wrongness of the universe" and humankind, and unconditionally accepts us as we are, assuring us of the relief of worthwhileness, forgiveness, and immortality.

This is the reason that, despite the prevalent popular notion to the contrary, there are two and only two kinds of religion in history. There are those that operate on the assumption that God is unconditionally for us and those that operate on the assumption that God is against us. The latter build intricate strategies in ethics and worship to provide techniques for self-justification. They are also shaped by a treadmill of strategies to placate the dangerous god they envision. The former express themselves in authentic celebration of God's grace and our appropriate gratitude. The latter is always struggling with the psychological bondage of a blind alley. The former afford the freedom of life as an open-ended creative quest in which every experiment in life, and its inherent risk of error—theological, moral, and spiritual—is ultimately safe: for "grace is greater than all our short-falls and failures."

In this regard a number of observations are suggested. First, in all the history of human religion, the religion of grace appeared only once: in the experience that came to Abraham in Genesis 12 and 17. A renewal of that vision appeared in the ministry of Jesus of Nazareth. Thus, in this regard the Judeo-Christian experience of faith is uniquely the religion of grace in its original forms. Both have departed markedly from that simple realization of God's utter good will toward us under all circumstances. It is, nonetheless, epitomized in the way Jesus of Nazareth handled people.

Second, all other religious forms in history have assumed a threatening god and are religions of self-justifying, god-placating strategies, to be religiously practiced by anxious humans. Most forms of Judaism and Christianity have lost their grip on the theology of radical grace and taken the form of god-placating ritual. Buddhism and Hinduism are often compared with Christianity, but in point of fact are strategies of Karma, meaning that grace is not the essence, but trying harder to get life right is the issue. These are essentially escapist programs to work out one's Karma until one achieves Nirvana, deliverance from life, indeed from existence itself. They are designed to avoid divine threat and the pain of the human enigma as soon as one possibly can. Judaism, Christianity, and Islam are action religions which are invested in actively taking charge of the responsibilities of life, to create a more effective world for humanity than life used to be. However, Islam has missed the theology of grace that was the vision of Abraham and Jesus. Eastern religions, on the other hand are essentially religions of withdrawal, focused on the individual and not society's values or social need like good sewers, water systems, and hygienic bathrooms, to say nothing of progress toward ideal civilized values.

Third, by the time of Jesus, Judaism had long since lost its clear clean vision of grace and had become a full-blown religion of law, conceiving of God as a threatening deity that needed to be propitiated by legalistic rituals. Likewise, by the fifth century after Jesus' day Christianity had lost its clear vision of the radical and unconditional character of grace personified in the teaching, ministry, and life of Jesus and had fallen into the crass legalistic paganism of a religion of self-justification and legalistic God-manipulation. Luther cut through the notion of God as a threat and recovered a radical trust in God's unconditional grace. However, it took Reformation Christianity less than two centuries to return a scholastic theology of legalistic ritual and ethical strategies designed as tools for human manipulation of a threatening God, to draw God into kindness to us that otherwise God would have spurned. We are becoming more efficient all the time in our natural human inclination to revert to our native paganism, driven by our inability to trust God and God's announcements of unconditional and universal grace.

Consequently, in the total history of religion, in historical Judeo-Christianity as well as all others, the psychological pathologies of massive anxiety must be taken as seriously as a stronger driving force in humans than our faith and trust in God. In evaluating Jewish and Christian worship ritual and ethical codes, biblical or extra-biblical, we must be honest and admit that the driving force of psychological anxiety is much stronger in us than the acknowledgement of divine revelation. Only thus can we separate the cultural and psychological garbage from the clear good news of grace in sacred scriptures of any sort; and in religious traditions of any kind.

For example, Jewish or Christian prayer or worship ritual which is designed to motivate God to do something benevolent for us which God would not have the good sense or presence of mind to do without our petition, assumes that God's grace is not unconditional and universal. Prayer and worship as celebration of gratitude for God's grace is a profoundly different thing. The difference is that between the pathological product of human anxiety and the profound Pauline perception that God is for us and not against us (Romans 8).

The sole recommendation for Judeo-Christian grace insight as the truth of God, moreover, is the fact that Abraham's insight and Jesus' message are the only solution for the inherent human predicament of distorting and pathological anxiety regarding the "wrongness of existence" and the silence of the "great absent One." Jesus is in history, indeed, at the hinge of history. His way of handling people affirms our worthwhileness and resolves anxiety into tranquility by the psychological dynamics of cherishing forgiveness and acceptance. Jesus, in the name of God, affirms us as we are, affording thereby the psychic freedom to become what we are potentially able to be, in body, mind, and spirit (psyche). That is our only chance for meaningful life—humanity being what it is.

PSYCHOLOGICAL UNDERSTANDING OF THE BIBLE

It is crucial to understand these issues from the operational and applied side before we formulate our conceptual models. I have been reflecting lately on how I can epitomize both the content and method of my work in psychological hermeneutics of scripture. I think I have been able to conceptualize it articulately. I operate with three basic laws that I think must reign in the field of biblical interpretation if one is to get at the essential biblical truth. They are as follows:

1. The first law of biblical hermeneutics: A correct interpretation of the Bible requires that we have achieved a sound theology of Scripture. It is necessary to separate the garbage from the gospel in the Bible in order to discern what the word of God really is in the biblical narratives. The garbage is the cultural-historical matrix in which the essential message is conveyed. The gospel is the clear word of grace which is conveyed, wherever it breaks out.

    My approach to the psychological hermeneutics of biblical themes and texts is to move from the operationally applied side to the theoretical conceptual models. That is why I said above that I have been reflecting lately on how I can epitomize both the content and method of my work in psychological hermeneutics of scripture. I think I have been able to conceptualize it articulately as follows.

2. The second law of biblical hermeneutics: That which, in the Bible, is psychospiritually destructive for persons, that is, the Living Human Document, is not the divine word. That which is psychospiritually constructive for persons and our world is the divine word of God. That word will always be a word about grace and can be discerned clearly and cogently in the biblical text.

3. The third law of biblical hermeneutics: Use of the psychological lens is essential for determining what in the biblical narratives is psychospiritually constructive and what is destructive for humanity and our environment, namely, the entire created order of things. The warrant for divine truth is that it is psychospiritually healing for humans and our world. Whether a word is *psychologically and spiritually* sound and constructive is the criterion for divine truth.

ELABORATION

1. That the word of God is always the word of grace is not arguable. It is simply the claim I make and its warrant is that *only it* heals and enhances human life and personality development.

2. In my model, God is, by definition, a God of thoroughly unconditional, radical, and universal grace. Any God that is not a God of such grace, is, by definition, not God, but is a monster. Any idea that any human conjures up of God as not by definition a God of grace is

corrupt, monstrous, and confused, because it demonstrably damages rather than heals us and our world.

3. God is subtle and not obvious in the world and in our experience. So we must take a psychological lens and a spiritual lens to look at the subtle intimations of God's presence and nature in history, our material world, life, and our personal experience. These subtle intimations include a) the mindfulness of creation, b) the benevolence of providence, c) the natural urge in all things toward beauty, d) the fact that unconditional acceptance and forgiveness is the only ultimate healing force in life, e) the fact that this kind of service of grace is precisely tailored to our central need for healing that sets us free for growth, and the fact that there is in our world and its history a proclivity to produce regularly persons that incarnate in a graphic way the epitome of this revealing and healing grace, perhaps as frequently as every generation.

4. The warrant for what is real and true is what works. Only the equation of grace works in the ultimate healing, growth, maturation, and wholeness for which we, humans, have the potential and to which we are, therefore, inherently destined.

5. Therefore, we must conclude that by definition God is a God of grace. The fact that only this definition of God works for our healing, growth, maturation, and wholeness, confirms that it is the only rational and psychospiritually authentic way to conceptualize God. All other conceptualizations are deficient, destructive, and hence, monstrous.

A couple of concluding observations are suggested by this line of thought. First, much of what goes for Judaic or Christian religion is psychological distortion or full-blown pathology. Pastors and professional counselors must be willing and able to differentiate critically between constructive spirituality and healing religious behavior, on the one hand, and psychopathology masquerading as authentic faith expression, on the other. Much of what goes for theological and ethical truth is constituted, not of the insights of grace but of the pathology of the psyche. This is not an easy course. Some years ago it seemed quite difficult to discern whether the experiences of charismatic Christians, which suddenly proliferated in the church in the 1970s, without denominational boundaries, was some kind of self-hypnosis or delusion, or whether it was the movement of the divine spirit. In the end, the only way to discern whether it was piety or pathology was to analyze whether the outcome proved to be spiritually meaningful healing or meaningless and destructive. Rigid fundamentalist Christianity, with its propositional notions of divine truth, and superficial charismatic Christianity, with its mystical fabrication, both proved to be pathological and destructive; the former in the direction of false rationalism and the latter in a false mysticism.

These substitutes for the grace themes of scripture and the spiritual peace-affording message of forgiving divine love are alternatives to the clear word of God in the Bible, and a manifestation of psychic pathology. They are unproductive psychological processes of sublimation and denial that ultimately stultify the achievement of true wholeness and healthy personhood.

Finally, it is obvious that the inherent human anxiety syndrome does not adequately account for the unique and crucial faith insights of authentic Judaism and Christianity. However, significant for Christians in counseling and the other helping professions is the realization that the human need addressed by the unique grace insight is, nonetheless, very much a product of that inherent anxiety. It is also a product of the pathological nature of many religious traditions which reinforce a culture of fear of a threatening God. We were, obviously, all created to celebrate the experience of living life, as it were, hand in hand with God as our empathic father. However, we are cast by our unresolved hunger for the meaning of things in life, into the predicament of having lost the touch of his hand.

That may just be what the terror of history amounts to. That may be the real dimension of our mystification and "confusion of face." The ancient Hebrew myth of the garden tragedy may be closer to truth than is history. Our common human terror and our common hope may well be as St. Augustine urged. "Thou hast made us for thyself, and out souls are restless until they rest, O God, in thee."

In any case, as those skilled to deal with psychic pathology, it is crucial that we keep clearly in focus the psychic source of human religion in the universal experience of profound anxiety about our very being and existence. That perspective is crucial to an intelligible discrimination and evaluation of the high incidence of *religious* complexities and fixations in neurotic and psychotic pathologies. Moreover, there is a high likelihood of direct relationship between anxiety as the source of religion, on the one hand, and the typical sex-religion disorder syndrome in mental illness, on the other. Sex, after all, is the second most anxiety-inducing phenomenon in human life, only after spirituality and its religious expressions. Furthermore, sexuality and spirituality, if traced back to their roots and central sources in the core of our being, are the same phenomenon, the same dynamic life force reaching out for the other human and for God.

It is crucial that authentic spiritual experience, religious expression, and psychic pathology are carefully differentiated. Then worship can be real and redemptively healing. Then spirituality can lead to the "fun and relief of being believers" (Rom 15:13), and not a bondage to fear of an angry God. Then life can be the experience of the freedom of grace.

5

The Biblical-Theological Underpinnings

IN HIS ADMIRABLE BOOK, *The Yahwist: The Bible's First Theologian*, Peter Ellis (1968) pointed out in a way that is very convincing that the main line of Jewish and Christian biblical theology is the message of God's radical, universal, and unconditional or uncalculating grace. That means that the Bible's story is founded upon the main stream of God's declared forgiveness for everybody, for everything, for evermore, as has been repeatedly made plain so far throughout this volume. Ellis observes that the first part of the Bible that Jews have long called the Torah is made up of many distinct narrative traditions. The Hebrew word, Torah, means God's word, law, message, or tradition. When the Old Testament was translated into the Greek language Torah became Logos. The gospel of John uses Logos to speak of God's self-expression or revelation. That New Testament use of Logos is translated as Word, and has the same meaning and weight as the Jewish use of Torah.

Torah refers to the first five books of the Bible, often called the Pentateuch. The many distinct and somewhat disparate stories that are woven together to form it are referred to in terms of the main characteristics of each. The narrative that refers to God as Yahweh is called the Yahwist tradition. That which refers to God as El or Elohim is named the Elohist tradition. Then there is the Priestly tradition that refers to that which was composed by the priests in Babylon during the exile (586–500 BCE). The rest of the story of the Torah is simply referred to as the Deuteronomic or Deuteronomistic narrative. With a trained eye for analysis of biblical texts

The Biblical-Theological Underpinnings

one can trace readily with considerable accuracy the theological strains of the Pentateuch.

The theological influence of these differing strains can be traced throughout all of the books of the Hebrew Bible. Furthermore, the famed interpreters of the New Testament, from ancient times, had little difficulty demonstrating that the life and ministry of Jesus personified and incarnated precisely the thrust of the message of the Yahwist theologian as he wrote the original story. Consequently the Christian scriptures became strong theological and pastoral expression of the practical message of God's radical grace.

Brevard Childs (1979) has done the world of biblical study a fine favor in writing his *Introduction to the Old Testament as Scripture*. He argues for a decreasing emphasis upon careful analysis of different traditions in biblical literature that have resulted from the scholarly editing in ancient times. He wants us to concentrate instead on the final product, the Bible as we have it. That is the book, after all, that has meant so much over the long centuries of its influence upon the spiritual, religious, and cultural life of Judaism, Christianity, and Islam. For Judaism and Christianity these scriptures have been loved and honored as the authoritative canonical revelation: God's word for the world.

Childs' book is a new watershed volume in biblical scholarship. Childs finds the tension between the biblical theology of unconditional grace and the conditionalism of the judgment passages to be more troublesome than do I. The overriding clarity of God's radical grace as the substructure of all scripture, OT and NT, is confirmed by Childs' emphasis on the Bible as the canon of the divine word.

The Bible sounds a clear and singular trumpet, whose notes convey singularly good news. It is the good news that first exploded uniquely into the Jewish theological tradition in Abraham's faith vision, and was captured pristinely by the Yahwist in Genesis 12 and 17. It is the good news that God accepts us as and where we are for the sake of what we can, therefore, become. It is the good news about healing and wholeness for the pathological, inadequate, distorted, and lost persons of this world that we all are. It is the word about the only chance for the likes of us.

In sum, the theology of grace asserts that God is in the enterprise of healing through forgiveness and consolation. Unconditional forgiveness for everyone, for everything, for evermore! That grace that is character-rooted in God, is radical in its incisive thrust to the central place of our pathology: the anxiety driven self-preoccupation that is both the cause and result of human alienation from God and God's ideal for us. It is the cause and result of the world of sickness and sin that devolves from that alienation. That grace is unconditional, because it is not merely something God does; but what God is. Hence it is an attribute and disposition inherent and inevitable in God.

The Yahwist would have us understand, moreover, that grace is universal in its scope and intent. The import is that humans are drawn by the Word to notice that the historical and empirical evidence available about the nature of God leads to a world view in which God's reason for existence, as humanly perceived, is the overt cultivation of the wholeness and wholesomeness of humans and of the whole creation. That is the essential reason why this book attempts to explore the psychological consequences of a thoroughgoing biblical theology of divine grace.

A proper assessment of the theological idea and its psychological import requires some exploration of the problematic and pathological nature of the human setting to which grace speaks, a clarification of how grace speaks to the human condition, and a consolidation of the conceptual base for drawing out the psychological consequences.

THE HUMAN PREDICAMENT

Since humans first sensed the radical and generic nature of our spiritual and psychological inadequacy or, on realizing our full psycho-spiritual potential, the most essential and universal human experience has been that of anxiety. As noted previously in this volume, Barbara Mertz expressed it as our common human terror and our common hope. Generic human anxiety is both systemic and situational for all persons. It is so radical in nature, that is, so close to the essence of our identity, that everything human is in some dimension shaped by it.

Eric Fromm (1997) adequately described the tragic side of its impact in human affairs in his book, *The Anatomy of Human Destructiveness*. John G. Finch has argued with considerable effect that generic human anxiety is also a potentially constructive dynamic in human growth. Seward Hiltner (1949) effectively related human anxiety and divine grace. Mertz seems accurate, therefore, in relating our generic anxiety to both our terror and our hope.

The Biblical-Theological Underpinnings

OUR TERROR

The terror dimension of anxiety is readily identified by and in us all. It ranges broadly from our struggle to come to terms with death and with our omnipresent mortality, to such forms of exaggerated anxiety as those that are usually identified as, or produce, the plethora of pathologies we clinically speak of as neuroses. From the moment that the uterine contractions, signaling impending birth, begin, until the last gasp of life's breath in enfeebled old age, life offers an overarching set of anxiety-inducing threats to the stability, goal achievement, fulfillment, and vital existence of life itself. The whole spectrum of life's experience process may be comprehensively and definitely described as a conscious and subconscious endeavor at gaining increasing control of one's destiny.

The native sense of psychological and spiritual brokenness universal to humans is surely rooted in that initial loss of paradaisical world of the womb, in which security is normally the overriding quality of experience. That loss is not experienced benignly but ingrains in our earliest and most essential precognitive, psychospiritual experience a sense of the essential violent and tragic character of life. That we ever achieve any genuine stasis and functionality after the birth trauma is really quite surprising. It is surely evidence of the divine gift of our resilient force of life and will.

The beginning of terrors is really the experience of being torn violently and painfully from that setting to which we are wholly adjusted, in that sense committed, and which we love systemically in the sense of being identified with, attached to, and dependent on it. Birth, therefore, means the loss experience, not merely of separation but of separation perceived as alienation. That alienation is experienced in conjunction with an overwhelming sense of fragileness, vulnerability, and disenfranchisement as we are cast out of the womb into the most alien world one can imagine. We find ourselves in the most abject helplessness and hopelessness which the experience of personhood could possibly offer. In terms of the classic dynamics of grief, that vulnerability is probably interpreted by the precognitive neonate as unworthiness. Our alienation from God and the godly, personally and as a community, reinforces all this sense of lostness.

It is of little surprise, therefore, that our sense of the authenticity of the biblical story of the Fall is so spontaneous. Genesis 3 accounts for, illumines, and interprets our most fundamental awareness: we are creatures of loss, a loss we experience and ultimately perceive as alienation and that feels like a state of powerlessness and unworthiness. Moreover those experiences and perceptions lie chronologically, logically, and psychologically so close to our origins and our essence that we sense them as definitive of our identity. We are not sinners so much as we are just sick and lonely. We are alienated and lost souls.

For Adam and Eve, in the mythic biblical story, created at full bloom and ensconced in the garden of paradise, the story of the Fall describes a psychospiritual experience akin to the general human trauma of birth, getting cast out of the womb, combined with the post-pubertal, oedipal-entrenched process of adolescent disengagement from parents and home, with all its inherent separation anxiety, ambivalence, and endangered certification.

In short, our common human terror is that of being wrenched from our mother's womb and being unable to catch hold of our father's hand. The essential psychological and spiritual experience is that of being orphaned, and as is always the case with children who experience pain and grief-loss, we internalize that sense of lostness, personally and communally, as guilt. That guilt ultimately produces anger, because the rationality of that guilt is almost impossible to identify, and the anger reinforces our sense of alienation, producing psychological and spiritual depression, distortions, pathologies, and hostile, inappropriate behavior. Here lies the threat of the loss of hope and loss of the meaningfulness and worthwhileness of things and is the engine driving our sin. That is the reason I claim that the problem of human dysfunction is sickness, not sin.

OUR HOPE

On the other hand, the separation experience of birth, as well as that of adolescent disengagement, brings with it the promise of hope. Both are pregnant with new possibilities. Birth brings a new breath of fresh air, as does the adolescent-young adult adjustment process and growth. In this the ontogeny of the person, so to speak, recapitulates the phylogeny of the cosmos.

In the biblical story, both the creation and the fall are oriented toward the future. Both are driven by the dynamics of expectation, both are filled with the potential of new life and a new world. The first is paradaisical, the second tragic, but in a certain essential sense, both are part of the birth process of the world of humanity. Both reach for the achievement of salvation and the completion and resolution of all things. The biblical story of creation, fall, and redemption is a historical paradigm of the universal human psychodynamic process of womb tranquility, birth trauma, adolescent disengagement and maturation. As in the paradigm, so in the psychology of the development of persons, the trauma of our genesis and the pain and risks of adolescence are drawn together into a comprehensive birth process from which the person comes, reaching consciously and subconsciously for the denouement of health and maturity with its healing resolution of things and its closures.

Now health and maturation, which I shall from this point comprehend in such terms as healing and wholeness, are achieved by stages, in fits and starts, with distortions, regressions and pathologies, hopeful surges and dead-end streets. This is not unlike the biblical paradigm in which God at various times, in bits and pieces, invested the fathers with salvation through the prophets and finally, in the end time, illumined and healed us through God's son (Heb 1:1). The whole process in the human person and in the paradigm of sacred history reaches hopefully forward expecting fulfillment of the total potential of wholeness inherent in God's image bearers and in God's cosmic experiment.

The whole of life and history, therefore, can be described as the process of trauma moving toward hope, tragedy driving to denouement, pained and distorted life reaching for wholeness, anxiety wanting reduction, dissonance longing for resolution.

ANXIETY REDUCTION AND HUMAN HEALTH

Since the whole process of personal and cosmic function moves from incompleteness and pathology (lostness, distortion, and palpable illness) to maturity and wholeness (health, fulfillment, and tangible salvation), the efficiency with which this is accomplished depends directly upon the effectiveness of the reduction of distorting obstructions. In the biblical historical paradigm for the cosmos and the human community, the reduction of obstructions has to do with the removal of the bonds of chaos in Genesis 1:1, of primitivity and naiveté in Genesis 1 and 2, and of idolatry in the rest of scripture. In the individualized psychodynamic odyssey of each person, the reduction of obstructions to wholeness involves anxiety reduction and thus transcendence over the pathology and distortions anxiety brings with it. Incidentally, in both the historical cosmic quest and the individual odyssey, wholeness is achieved ultimately *sola gratia* (by grace alone) but not *sola Deo gloria* (only for the glory of God). Because grace is grace, the wholeness that it brings is, through incarnation, for the creation. It is God's forgiving and affirming reach for humanity and its well being. History, the Bible, and sound psychotherapy, for example, are in that sense human-centered. God, theology, and Christian psychology, when authentically perceived and expressed, are for, and preoccupied with, suffering persons and a suffering world (worlds).

Anxiety-reduction processes in the odyssey of personal growth may, of course, be constructive or destructive. I am convinced that all distortions, pathologies, and dead-end streets (self-destructive courses) in human psychospiritual development are the consequences of a destructive anxiety-reduction mechanism at the level of the psyche or at the level of social function or both. Conversely, wholesome growth, health, and maturation are achieved to the degree that constructive anxiety-reduction mechanisms are introduced and utilized. Time and space do not permit an exploration here of the fall as Adam's constructive or destructive anxiety-reduction method for the anxiety-laden and hopeful quandary with which he struggled, regarding his potential to be like God, knowing good and evil. But that is a dimension of this matter that requires carefully psycho-theological analysis if one is to be biblically and theologically sound. It is, therefore, treated at length in chapter six. Destructive anxiety-reduction methods are those that produce inhibitory defensive processes in human growth. Constructive anxiety-reduction mechanisms are those that enhance the openness for assertive risk-taking processes in human growth. The former obstruct, delay, distort, limit, or sicken and thus prevent the efficient move toward total self-actualization as an image bearer of God, whose destiny it is to realize palpable fulfillment of our psychospiritual potential. Constructive anxiety-reduction mechanisms support, direct, reinforce, equip, embellish, and expand the human person and thus promote the efficient move toward total self-actualization. That realization of human growth and destiny in the fulfillment of the full range of the psychospiritual potential with which God has invested each of us is the very definition of health and wholeness.

Every function or behavior designed to bring that about is a healing act and the very definition of healing. All our sickness and our sinfulness is thus a falling short of the glory of God, because it is an obstruction of God's glorious ambition for us, a falling short of achieving the glory of real humanness. Functionality and dysfunction have their meaning against that backdrop, and that divine ideal.

THE ROLE OF RELIGION

The history of religion is the history of the human endeavor to devise functional anxiety-reduction mechanisms capable of managing situational and systemic anxiety: life shaping angst. That long religious history divides easily into two radically opposite camps, shaped by differing strategies for anxiety reduction. The most prominent camp, historically, is the one shaped by the anxiety-reduction strategy of human achievement: measuring up to psychosocial standards of function that then authorize self-justification. This is essentially a strategy of self-justification by achievement of an ethical or psychosocial power position. It is self-centered and self-directed, and tends to be legalistic and mechanistic. It is not growth oriented but status oriented, and since it treats only one superficial behavior, it deals only with the symptoms of our failed humanness. The generic human anxiety is never effectively reduced. Thus it is in the end self-defeating. It cannot cut through to the heart of our essential lostness and the orphaned nature of human persons.

This kind of religion may provide a pseudo-womb-return experience, such as some forms of institutionalized religion provide, but it never puts the grasping human hand back into the hand of our Father. In this strategy God remains the adversary who must be placated, outflanked, intimidated, or manipulated. God becomes a projection of the anxiety-laden and guilt-ridden psyche of the religionist whose unworthiness drives him or her to worship or works-righteousness. This religious strategy for anxiety reduction produces and enhances psychopathology.

With one exception, religions throughout human history fall into this first camp, anxiety reduction by human achievement, a strategy for placating God. They constitute a psycho-religious power-play schema, designed to control God who is imagined to be dangerous and a threat. Such religion produces the psychopathology and spiritual distortions inherent in that kind of defense mechanisms. It is an attempt to manage God to keep God from doing too much damage to us.

GOD'S GRACE

The only exception to this general psychospiritual tragedy of human history is the unique Judeo-Christian theology of God's radical, unconditional and uncalculating, universal grace: forgiveness for everybody, for everything, for evermore. It is precisely the theology of the Yahwist, the Bible's first theologian. It comes to flower in Jesus Christ and Paul's New Testament perspectives. That is the only healing option. Only here is religion a constructive anxiety-reduction instrument.

The theology of the Yahwist is such a healing option, because it cuts through to the heart of our essential lostness and orphaned nature. It is not a theology of self-justification but of unconditional divine acceptance. It is not a strategy for an ethical or psychosocial power play for manipulating God, but a way of self-acceptance. It is not self-directed but goal-directed toward the completion of the whole person in faith, hope, and health. It is not mechanistic or legalistic but dynamic, growth oriented, not status oriented.

This way of life mollifies some of the pain of our symptoms of psychospiritual unwholesomeness and inadequacy to the responsibilities of life and the challenges of godliness. It treats the dis-ease and disease of our sense of alienation from God, falling short of God's glorious possibilities for us. It does not lead us back to the womb but puts our hand in the hand of our Father, not back to paradise but ahead to paradise. When properly mediated, the Yahwist grace perspective of Genesis 12 and 17 heals human pathology in mind and spirit. It is, in fact, the most comprehensive and relevant psychological theory and practice ever conceived, divine acceptance and affirmation of us all, just where we are right now in our pilgrimage, for the sake of what we can become when freed from all the sickening forces of fear, guilt, and shame. I am thoroughly convinced that everyone who really hears this message in the inner ear of the heart will automatically and inevitable turn his or her face toward God and declare, "If that is the way God feels about me, I want to be God's kind of person."

The God of Abraham, Isaac, and Jacob; of David, Isaiah, and Micah; the Judeo-Christian God we know in Jesus, John, and Paul is not a threat but our ultimate consolation. God's name is Yahweh, the faithful one, the covenanting God of promises that are kept, who by the meaning of God's name and by God's nature guarantees that God will be for us and not against us, as he has always been for humankind. That name is, therefore, a strong tower of security. "The righteous run into it and are safe" (Prov 18:10b).

The Biblical-Theological Underpinnings

Righteous means, according to David (Ps 32 and 51), Micah (7:18–20), and Paul (Rom 8), that person whom God has unconditionally accepted and to whom God has imputed righteousness: all of us human beings.

Unfortunately, superficial reading of the history of Judaism and Christianity will not confirm the radical uniqueness of that tradition of constructive anxiety-reduction. By the heyday of Davidic Israel, a pagan legalism and mechanistic atonement theology were already rampant, the notion that one should pay for ones failings and placate God. Christ cut through to the essence of the grace theology, but by the fifth century of the Christian era the seeds of a pagan legalism were again sown; by the eighth century a sturdy growth was evident; and by the eleventh century it had fruited. Luther grasped the essence of grace once again, though scholasticism had demeaned Protestant grace theology two centuries later.

At the personal level, even in the best of times, popular religion has usually remained extensively threat-motivated paganism, despite the quality of the church's theology and ministry. Furthermore, in each generation there seems to arise a new form of Christian paganism that manifests itself in popular ecclesiastical movements that are essentially anxiety inducing or pathogenic in their anxiety-reduction methods. The fastest growing churches tend consistently to be those that appeal to theologically untutored communities with notions that foster simplistic constructs of legalistic anxiety-management—in essence strategies of self-righteousness and salvation by personal discipline and good works.

That stands against the gospel of grace and the theology of the Yahwist. The substance of the Yahwist document itself is essentially that of the story of creation, and the good news of Genesis 3:15 (all pathology will be crushed), and the covenant with Abraham for the healing of all nations. These seeds of grace are enacted through the Exodus and the promise of Davidic *Shalom*. The theology hinges, of course, on the creation, the fall, and the covenant. The central factor consistent throughout is the status of humanity. In that mythic narrative Adam appears on the scene as the special imager of the divine nature in a divinely ordered world. The God-imaging quality of humanity in the creation story describes the essential nature and character of humans.

David J. A. Clines (1968) urges us to take this seriously enough to recognize that the doctrine elevates all humankind to the highest status conceivable, "short of complete divinization." In that divinely ordered world, Adam is assigned the stature and status of compatriot of God. That status describes, not his essential nature as imager, but his role and relationship with God. Adam keeps the garden, names the animals, seeks a mate, receives Eve as God's gift for appropriate communion, and walks with God in the cool of the evening. His status is imputed to him by God, arbitrarily. The story never refers to Adam as son of God or child of God or servant of God. He is portrayed consistently as companion and compatriot of God. Moreover, that status is a covenant status, not negotiated by Adam but in the style of the Mesopotamian regents, imputed and guaranteed by God.

In that early biblical myth, part of Adam's wholesome character as compatriot of God is the quality of his imagination. He can imagine alternative worlds, alternative models of relationship, alternative perceptions of the good for which to quest, even evil perceptions of the good, and other anxiety-inducing possibilities, options and challenges. When Adam selected the alternative option of independence, the childlike harmony of his universe metamorphosed into a dissonance and discordance that, but for grace, would have been deadly to the extent that it increasingly amplified Adam's alienation from the garden, the God-walks, his wife-talks, his own tranquility, and his own true destiny as a person in whom all the rich potential for wholeness could be actualized.

The deadly dynamic in that independent course was the potential for overwhelming anxiety increase, to the point at which Adam would have been consumed by coping with his lostness, his inability to grasp again his Father's hand. Adam's status of God-compatriot seemed hopelessly forfeited, and his course of behavior seemed at fundamental odds with his own essential nature as an imager of God. *It was almost as though his God-imaging nature as independent creator was in tension with his God-compatriot nature of co-keeper of the garden.* That dissonance was the potential for sickness and death in the fall.

The crucial issue, of course, is this: When Adam "fell" God, despite his declaration "you shall surely die", refused to change Adam's essential status as God-compatriot. It was an arbitrarily imputed status. Now it is an arbitrarily maintained status. Adam's life now has about it the deadly pathological possibilities of overwhelming alienation, lostness, distortion, dissonance, sickness, and sin. Nonetheless, God came to Adam, sat where he sat, and adopted the new circumstances of Adam's life as the new arena for their relationship. God made clear immediately the unconditional nature of the compatriot status, and proceeded with the original business of Adam's move toward wholeness, completeness, growth, and healing. The ground rules where somewhat modified, the trajectory of Adam's destiny now started at a different place. He was outside the garden, with all the symbolism that implied. However, the change was only in terms of the new requirements for constructive anxiety reduction: God's declaration of conflict between the human pursuit of humanity's destiny and the presence of evil in history (Gen 3:15) and the human reach toward the divine reassurance (Gen 12:1–4 and 17:1–8), "I will bless you ... and you will be a blessing ... and by you shall all the families of the earth be blessed."

The critical element of the theology of grace, throughout scripture, in consequence, is the essential inviolability of that status arbitrarily imputed by God for humanity and faithfully maintained by God for the whole human race. We cannot sin ourselves out of God's grace. We cannot squirm out of God's long embrace. In the tragedy of our anxiety we perceive lostness and alienation. Out of that comes our sickness and our sin, psychologically and spiritually. From God's perspective, however, our status is unchanged. We are unconditionally affirmed as those destined for communion with God as a way of life, and self-actualization as our destiny as image bearers of God's own nature and self.

HUMAN HEALTH

The predicament of human existence, thus, is not our lostness but our perceived lostness. Our destiny is not that of achieving a successful power play to "get right with God" or to get the right leverage with God. Our destiny is to accept and realize the benefits of our status: compatriots of God, companions with God in the quest for wholeness and health, and co-laborers with God in keeping our community and God's world wholesome and safe. The benefits are the relief of grace, the affirmation of our real selves, our unconditional acceptance of God's unconditional acceptance of us, and the celebration of our generic freedom from the need for generic anxiety: systemic ("Fear not, I am thy God") and situational ("Be anxious in nothing. Take no thought for the morrow").

It is not surprising then, that Paul, in developing the rudiments of a Christian anthropology, should speak of primordial man, fallen man, and the man in Christ. Hans Dieter Bets (1989, cf. also 1985) points out that there is an apparent tension in Pauline anthropology between Paul's classical Greek humanistic roots and his classical Yahwist roots. Paul worries greatly about the role of the law, the need for the suppression of the lower passions by the higher, the body (*sarx*—animal instincts) held in check by the spirit (*psyche*). Here he has the Greek split of the human into body, mind, and spirit, with the former warring against the latter in humans. Yet he is radical in his "free grace theology" and the doctrine of imputed righteousness (Rom 8; Eph 2:1–10). Here Paul's Hebrew roots in the unified model of humans in which we are made in God's image, genitals and all. So there is not tension between the lower and higher passions. They are both created and affirmed by God and are good and glorious aspects of our life with God.

J. Christiaan Beker (1980) resolved that paradox in a delightful way in his book, *Paul the Apostle,* by demonstrating conclusively that Paul never intends to write a systematic theology, not even in Romans. Paul's model of human nature, his anthropology, comes down to Yahwist theology and our imputed status in God's grace. That is the supremely relevant constructive anxiety-reduction mechanism of all history. It addresses the essential angst behind all psychopathology and spiritual disorder. It is the essential insight for healing and wholeness for the likes of us.

Some exciting recent studies of the biblical theology of grace invite the attention of psychologists today. Karl Barth (1957), of course broke the theology of grace out of the medieval prison of scholastic categories with his stimulating existentialist theology of election. James Daane's book, *The Freedom of God* (1973) is a lucid step beyond Barth, in the tradition of Paul. Daane's work is a theology of the triumph of God, hammered out on the situational anvil of parish preaching. Daane defeats scholasticism with its time-bound God and secular philosophical teleology by rooting salvation in election, as does Barth, in the historical and existential function of Jesus Christ. Donald Bloesch (2010) says of Daane that he "persuasively argues that election is grounded in the free decree of God that is historical as well as eternal, and that has its culmination in Jesus Christ." Niel Punt's (1980) *Unconditional Good News* argues that Yahwist and Pauline theologies import clearly that in Jesus Christ all humanity is elected by God to grace and forgiveness, unconditionally, and that the redemptive consequences of that do not leave anyone out.

Though these do not go far enough in understanding grace, they take great strides toward a thoroughgoing theology of grace that can illumine our essential nature as God-compatriots. More recently I have developed this biblical notion of the unconditional grace of God in a series of three volumes entitled, *A Dangerous Report* (2012), *God's Radical Grace* (2012), and *By Grace Alone: Forgiveness for Everyone, for Everything, for Evermore* (2013). These carry forward in popular form my book written especially for pastors and therapists, entitled *Radical Grace, How Belief in a Benevolent God Benefits Our Health* (2007). As the radical, unconditional, and universal nature of the biblical message of God becomes clearer to the theologians, their service to psychologists and vice versa will substantially increase. Psychologists understand with increasing attentiveness: 1) our fallenness or brokenness as the source of human psychopathology; 2) the healing dynamic of incarnated grace, called by Carl Rogers unconditional positive regard (1965); 3) the relationship between the clinical function and the divine paradigm behind it; and 4) the manner in which this essentially theological anthropology must shape theoretical and applied psychology. Only then can we really understand how we are to handle humans authentically. The service of such psychologists to the theologians will thus be greatly enhanced regarding this very matter of defining and explicating grace. Perhaps Aquinas was right in his notion that the insight and illumination to which we have come by faith in divine revelation we would have come to anyway, if we had been able to track only the empirical evidence of human nature to its center by a careful and thorough science of psychology.

One might, indeed should, raise the point that my emphasis upon anxiety and its related psychological disorders applies only to psychopathologies that are purely psychodynamic and are not associated with chemical disorders, the latter being a large percent of what we see in the clinical setting. I acknowledge the relevance of this question. However, the evidence is increasing that the two-way switching function of the hypothalamus urges us to consider that anxiety and our sense of the loss of meaning may even there be the pathogenic factor.

Secular and humanist psychology has provided valuable insights regarding symptomology, dynamics, and central disorders of the human psyche and soul. Empirical research into characterological and personality disorders and their biochemical links has achieved profound depth and precision. Strategies generally in use for management of psychopathologies have great value. Christian perspective, however, is indispensable in illumining the root cause and cure for our common human terror and our common hope.

6

The Psychodynamics of the Fall Story

INTRODUCTION

THE STORY OF THE fall of human beings into the sin of prideful disobedience recorded in the Hebrew Bible is intriguing from numerous points of view. Whether it is understood literally, metaphorically, mythically, or symbolically, the story provokes a spontaneous and universal sense of its authenticity. It is one of those stories that carries with it such an archetypical quality that we sense at once that it touches, at the center, the generic truth of obvious human history and of definitive personal experience. It speaks of the radical tragic distance between what we can imagine as our ideal potential as persons and what we know as our often defeating and dissonant experience in real life.

The story is intriguing because, though it is woven into the fabric of the biblical literature, it is in fact, dependent for its formal elements upon an archaic Mesopotamian source. The role of the virgin, the tree, the fruit, and the phallic serpent as tempter, are imported with a little tailoring from pagan fertility literature. Though the story is not explicitly sexual, it is the story of a contest between two potential lovers seeking the allegiance of the virgin, a double seduction, the response of guilt, and the shame of sexual vulnerability and manipulation.

The story is equally intriguing for the manner in which the Hebrew editors attempted to adapt it for biblical theological use. Their key difference is the obvious literary effort to make the story fit and reveal something

The Psychodynamics of the Fall Story

essential about the manner in which God relates to the impaired universe and to the fractured human community, as we experience it existentially.

THE FUNCTION OF THE STORY

Related to this is the implication in the story of the general problem of evil. Clearly this foreign material is inserted into the fabric of the Hebrew Bible to assist in completing the biblical story of how the problem of evil arose in human life. It is designed to establish a base line for dealing with the problem as humans suffer it. The first such story to be borrowed and reedited for the Bible was Genesis 6, but that story makes God responsible for the problem of evil in the world. Genesis 3 was injected into the Bible by the editors during the exile (586–500 BCE) to claim that humans are to blame. The claim is that proud egotism led humans beyond their appropriate boundaries and landed them in such an erroneous position that God's design for nature and communion with humans was disrupted and alienated. The flowering shrubs began to look like thorns, the walks with God began to look like a threat, and the complexity of human relationships began to look like a thicket of unmanageable confusion and pain.

The fall story endeavors to account for the problem of human suffering in body, mind, and soul; and the universal disorder in the world. It attempts to explain why humans can conceive of aesthetic ideals but hardly create them, long for a perfect world but not fashion one, hope for genuine love but seldom express or experience it, remember and anticipate paradise yet sense it always eluding us.

It is an intensely pathetic story of loss, grief, guilt, and shame. The pathos of the story is equally significant in revealing the essential nature of the universal human predicament, whether the story is understood as history or as myth. The literary characteristics strongly suggest, of course, that it should be viewed as a mythical story so invested with theological content and import as to be profoundly true in what it intends to say about our humanness. It is a mythic narrative but it is truer than mere historical reporting could ever possibly be. The truth it articulates is that of the general state of brokenness humans universally experience, expressed in their pervading distortion, debilitating anxiety, and apparent "wrongness" of human existence.

The story may be helpfully viewed as a theological myth, imported into the sacred canon by the Hebrew believers, but taken from Mesopotamian sources for the purpose of describing the psychological state of affairs they perceived to afflict humanity. They saw themselves and the human race as alienated, orphaned, and diseased. The truth of course is not that we have fallen from a perfect state of paradise for which we were created, but that, while we have achieved great advances in the span of human existence, we are still not far enough advanced from the Chimpanzees, our ancestors with whom we share 98% of our DNA. Nonetheless, the Hebrew editors were right about one thing. We are people who fall short of the potential ideal for which God has created us. We are inadequate for the responsibilities of life and the challenges of godliness.

The fall is an element in a cosmic paradigm for the general state of human psychological development. It describes a crucial stage in human growth from the childhood of Eden to the mature work in God's world, with cultural and spiritual responsibility. In that growth process, the story plays the role for the human race that corresponds to the adolescent process for individuals: the psychosocial movement through individuation, separation, and independence from supervisory authority to maturity. Those separation processes are normally fraught with significant anxiety. That stress is also evident in the story of the fall, as the players, Adam and Eve, react to the events of the narrative. The tension of adolescence is about the fear, guilt, and shame associated with the new sense of vulnerability as we move beyond the hovering care of parents.

The tension and anxiety is related to the actors' increasing awareness of the exciting and dangerous presence of the forbidden tree, their perception of the possibility of making a dangerous decision, the new state of affairs represented by the tempting serpent, the seduction of Eve, and the familiar move of her seduction of Adam. These strange new anxiety-inducing elements in the previously uncomplicated childlike safety of the garden, are internalized the way children always internalize anxiety. The anxiety causes the internal dissonance of fear, guilt, and shame. We are aware of the radical new world we create for ourselves as we cut loose from parents. The entire fabric of life is torn open as we move to the stage of independent and responsible maturity.

In fact, the most interesting element is the plain implication that a significant sense of danger and its inherent state of anxiety existed in the human experience before the fall. While paradise was still intact Adam and Eve were disturbed by the God-induced dissonance caused by setting them before the choice of reverting to their childishness of Eden, and the growth in becoming more like God in whose image they were made and intended to flourish. That required understanding both good and evil instead of merely the naiveté of children. They were challenged with trying the fruit of the tree. What an interesting experiment on the part of God.

Our acknowledgment of the state of anxiety that existed in the life and spirit of humans, before the decision for maturity instead of naiveté, gives us the clue as to how this narrative is to be properly interpreted. Adam and Eve did not fall down the stairs. They stumbled up the stairs to new heights of responsibility, work, care, culture-building, and communion with God. This is an important insight into essential human nature that the Hebrew editors apprehended. It implies the need in Adam (humans), as he was created, for an anxiety-reduction mechanism that would make it possible for him to cope and to open the door of his own primitive and childlike life to real growth. He was challenged to accept his God-given potential as a full-fledged person. He had a growth-oriented destiny, and so did his whole world, in God's creative design. To be God's whole person he needed to accept the challenge that would bring him and humanity to the full realization and expression of being persons, reaching for their ideal God-given potential.

As soon as God announced the presence and import of the dangerous tree, a state of anxiety was unavoidable. Adam and Eve perceived that their potential destiny was open-ended, their truth was open-ended. This required decision-making by them if they were to realize themselves as persons. They recognized that they possessed the potential for change and for negative or positive growth. Their anxiety increased in intensity as the story recounts their struggling with the essential decision. It was the challenge of moving into their unknown future. Moreover, the pressure of that anxiety is further increased as they contemplate, quite correctly, the possibility of being like God, open to all truth and reality about themselves and God's world.

It should not surprise us that the story describes the Garden of Eden as anxiety laden. Stress in the pre-fall state, as described in this psycho-theological myth, is already evident much earlier. Adam is described as finding himself alone in the garden in a state of sufficient disequilibrium that he looked for a mate or companion among the animals. He found none adequate or appropriate. God noted the stress and anxiety and intervened by creating Eve as a help appropriate to his neediness. Obviously that means that she filled out some condition of lack and anguish in Adam and thereby reduced his stress and anxiety.

One can imagine that Adam, as the main character in this story, had considerable stress from numerous directions in that paradise: from the pressure of responsibility to keep the garden, responsibility to find companionship that was appropriate, to name the animals, to fashion a meaningful relationship with his wife, who ultimately chose a liberation course of independence and then seduced him into following her, presumably lest he lose her, and finally responsibility to obey and love God in a world where the manner of doing that held some ambiguity. The man was under pressure!

Adam's anxiety, in the story, is not the consequence of his purported sin. His anxiety is clearly the result of his being a person with unexplored potential and possibilities. It is inherent to his nature and all human nature. It is inevitable to human existence, because of the nature of the potential for growth and the unfolding unknown that growth and the freedom to grow involve. The Hebrews saw that and related it to the potential in the world for the problem of our human travail. So they told the old Mesopotamian story in a new way and captured so precisely a truth generic to our existence that when we read the story five or six thousand years later, we find it touching the center of our predicament in some fundamental ways.

The story suggests that all this stress and anxiety that Adam experienced was finally culminated in the enigma of what to do about the possibility of being like God. The narrative of the fall, as the Hebrews understood it, describes the event and Adam's decision as his anxiety-reduction method, designed to free his psyche for further function, coping, and growth. The critical question, therefore, must be raised as to whether the event was a constructive or destructive anxiety-reduction mechanism for Adam and the human race. We ask the same question when we consider whether the painful process of birth and of adolescent disengagement is a constructive or destructive anxiety-reduction mechanism. It is important because it will give us some clues as to whether we are to look at human alienation, pain, and anxiety, together with its consequences as difficult but inevitable stages in the evolution of persons and the human community, or as an unfortunate aberration of a sinful or, at least, destructive type, as the Hebrews suggested.

BOISEN, BERRY, CLINEBELL, AND HILTNER

Seward Hiltner (1963) contended persuasively that the biblical story of the fall is a metaphor of the human process of maturing to individuality and responsible agency as persons. He, therefore, urged that the story is a report on the human psychological process of asserting the will of the human being against the will of God. He claimed that the act was necessary for humankind and is necessary for an individual, because saying "yes" to God is a commitment to being a Christian and builder of the divine reign in the earth, and it has no meaning or content if it is impossible to say "no."

Maturity for humanity, as for children, requires the ego strength and volition that forges the power and right to disengage from parent, even the divine parent, in order to give significance to the intent or behavior of commitment to that relationship at a mature level of function. Hiltner's notion reflects the paradigm of adolescent disengagement and assumes that it requires a willful negative act, testing one's own strength over against one's parent, general authority, or pressures toward conformity. Without this disengagement there can be no growth or maturity.

C. Markham Berry (1980b) suggested a similar perspective in pointing out that childhood is a stage of fusion with mother or parents. It moves progressively toward differentiation and achieves that with dramatic contrast in adolescence. Once the differentiation is successfully established and genuine individuality is achieved, there follows a process of return toward union, commitment, cherishing, and a new kind of fusion. Berry and Hiltner seem to support the contention of this chapter that the story of the fall represents that growth step of differentiation and disengagement which makes an authentic relationship with God a possibility.

It is not quite as clear whether the story of the fall describes a step taken in the best possible manner in which it might have been done. The narrative is cast in the form of an outright rebellion of humans against a specific directive from God. Howard Clinebell (1979) appears to emphasize that the negative aspects of human nature are elements or stages in an evolutionary continuum of growth. One would imagine that he would find in the Hebrew fall story an interesting and entertaining metaphor, but one of little significance as to whether it represents a real disengagement from God, and from the infantile state of paradise, for the sake of human growth toward discipleship or, in fact, comments in any other meaningful way upon the real existential nature of the human predicament. In the latter case, the Hebrew story would merely be a way of explaining mythically, in retrospect, why things are so difficult and turbulent in human life. He seemed to think that healthy adolescent growth moves more or less consistently along a line from primitivity, or childhood, to maturity, without the sort of psychological discontinuity that the fall story of painful adolescent disengagement represents in persons and in the history of the human race.

Anton Boisen (2015) actually set the stage for the perspectives of Hiltner, Clinebell, and Berry, by his argument that health in humans is always worked out from the resources that failure and illness bring to our struggle for growth, healing, and maturity. Boisen, himself, suffered six episodes of severe psychosis in his life. Each of these he considered to have been a turning point in his achievement of health and growth. He managed, quite surprisingly, to enter into his own psychotic experiences and face the dynamics of their dissonance and dysfunction in such a way as to dig deeply into their sources and use the forces he found there, in the causes of his illness, as the building blocks of finding health.

As a result, he was able to develop a theory and method for pastoral care of the mentally ill that became the core dynamic of the standard practice in the field of chaplaincy, clinical treatment, and pastoral psychology today. He disliked the concept of psychotherapy because he perceived that health was not achieved by removing the pathology or dysfunction, but by employing the disorder and the resources for growth and health. He felt that the counselor's role was not to deliver the counselee from the pain but to help him or her discern how to use it for growth, health, and maturity. Boisen's understanding of the fall story would be that it was a necessary and advantageous experience which enhanced human movement from real dysfunction to existential coping and health.

CONSTRUCTIVE OR DESTRUCTIVE

If the adolescent disengagement from parents is seen as paradigmatic of the fall story, or *vice versa*, it is useful to ask whether Adam might have done it in any better way. Does humanity need to express so much disjunction and experience so much alienation and loss in order to achieve mature personhood and growth? Was it a constructive or destructive anxiety-reduction method?

It is tempting to say that Adam and Eve chose the best course, and in view of their limited knowledge and experience, the only one they really had available to them. That is a way of saying that the loss and alienation we all experience from the loss of the womb and from adolescent individuation process, together with the distortion in the intra-psychic and psychosocial world that drives our sickness and our sin, is virtually inevitable. As

The Psychodynamics of the Fall Story

we grow, our limited knowledge, experience, and wisdom prevent us from choosing other than the painful and, at least temporarily, alienating course. Such an hypothesis would manage most of the relevant data neatly: this hypothesis implies that pain was inevitable, that the choice would not have been different if growth and maturation were to evolve out of the primitive and childlike naïveté of the Eden-womb.

It is clear, however, that the formulators of the Hebrew edition of this myth intended to explain the problem of evil and human disorder by asserting that humanity made a bad choice. That does not imply that some decisive act by Adam and Eve to move them from naïveté to maturity was not necessary. Neither does it mean that nothing constructive toward real growth came out of their decision. It only contends that the decision may have been a transitional act that was unnecessarily fraught with self-defeating pride, rebellion, and alienation. The Hebrews saw it as a destructive anxiety-reduction mechanism, insofar as they sensed it in those terms at all.

If one posits the notion that the fall story represents a destructive method of anxiety reduction for leading characters in the myth, and paradigmatically represents the disorder and alienation in the general human process of maturing, it suggests that our general response to the generic anxiety of birth and adolescent individuation is essentially destructive and self-defeating. That does not, however, erase the fact that the fall has a constructive, freedom-affording result for humans. Similarly, adolescence may be handled unnecessarily rebelliously by some teen-agers but lead out to a growth process that results in a profoundly wholesome re-fusing with parents or authorities in the long run, and a healthy relationship with the adults and their values and traditions later on. Paul seems to imply something of this regarding humanity when he ties the primordial state of human "bliss" into a continuum with the "fallen human" and the fruition of it all in the "new person in Christ."

The fall story represents one option of implementing the necessary and inevitable differentiation process. The Hebrews thought of it as a destructive option. The implication is that Adam and Eve might have exercised an equal growth-inducting act of will and ego strength by choosing, for independent and personal reasons, to affirm God's will and value system. Perhaps that could have been as initiatory, independent, and disengaging an act toward growth as disobedience proved to be. Presumable it would, moreover, have had less self-defeating, though adequately self-affirming consequences. Moreover, the paradigmatic import for human history is the implication that the distortion, pain, alienation, and sickness with which humans have responded to generic anxiety throughout history were not inevitable elements of the growth process of the race.

Perhaps we could be less inclined to solve all our ultimate problems of relationship and ego anxiety by immediate resort to the ultimate violence or war, as has been the history of the USA and of most peoples throughout the long stretch of time, as far back as we can reach. Humans have made many bad decisions: in the way we have perceived each other as threats, in the way we have apprehended God's real disposition to us, in the way we have responded to quandary and ambiguity, and in the degree of finesse with which we have carried out our own psychological dynamics and destiny. Such decisions, perhaps, can be made more wisely, redemptively, and faithfully, with healthier outcome.

The disengaging adolescent can achieve health and growth while choosing, as an independent act of will and ego, to affirm and follow the healthful values of parents, authorities, traditions, or other sources of encouragement toward conformity. Indeed, that course, when it expresses rather than compromises the child's own authenticity, may be far less self-defeating, inefficient, erosive of health, and less painful than individuation that strains relationships or maximizes confrontation, alienation, grief, and loss.

The Hebrews, however, stood in the existential situation of realizing that human life is painfully dysfunctional in many ways. They wanted to reach back and create a myth that would explain that. The story of the fall is a theological mythology that confesses that the meaning of human pain and disorder, in the face of God's kind providence and universal grace, is the result of a human mistake. This story gets God off the hook, so to speak. That was necessary for them because they already had a mythic story that blamed God for the disorder, pain, and dysfunction in the world. That story is recorded in Genesis 6 and was written long before Genesis 3. Genesis 6 is a revamped Mesopotamian narrative that says evil came into the world from the heavenly realm, making God the culprit.

Hiltner and Berry were correct in emphasizing the inevitable necessity of our differentiation from a womb-like or cradle-like relationship with God. It appears that the Hebrews were correct in implying that the individuation could be less self-defeating and could still affirm the perspective and value system that heals, rather than aggravates the generic human anxiety that so sickens us. Perhaps Clinebell was really on the right track in de-emphasizing the cataclysmic and alienating dimension of human "fallenness" while placing all the emphasis on the freedom for growth that humans as independent agents need and posses. His model handles the data in a way that implies that the fall speaks of a revolution and that, however paradigmatic that may be of actual human experience, humankind has the alternative option of evolutionary growth response to human anxiety.

It is intriguing to consider the possibility of humanity in general, and children in particular, developing through a peaceful, relatively non-turbulent adolescent exploration of the possibilities of being like God or parents, knowing good and evil.

My initial perspective in wrestling with the fall story in relationship to God's grace and human health was to conclude that Adam and Eve had no alternative. I was strongly inclined to the notion that turbulent and alienating process is inherent to adolescence and its disengagement, as well as to being born, and so the mythic couple's action seemed to me to be the only constructive anxiety-reduction mechanism they had available to free them toward health and growth.

I am indebted to my daughter for persuading me to rethink that. The idea at the center of this chapter is really her argument that the fall story represents an unnecessarily self-destructive form of adolescent rebellion. Presumably Adam and Eve could have developed and made the transition to maturity tranquilly and constructively, leaving the garden and becoming responsible builders of wholesome culture in God's world. That is a real possibility for healthy and cherishing adolescents. That seems clearly to be what the Hebrew editors intended to say. What urged me to take a new look at that matter was the increasing success of my daughter's struggle to disengage by evolution rather than by revolution. She refused assiduously to give up that course of cooperative exploration to maturity, even when I was betimes less than useful to her constructive, exploratory growth. To this day, however, I continue to wonder what that may have cost her in pain and travail.

Disengagement by evolutionary and constructive anxiety reduction has worked for her, at whatever emotional cost, and for me also, at whatever cost. It struck me in thinking about this that the odyssey of Jacques Cousteau's son must have been a little like the experience of me and my daughter. Instead of "running away to sea," literally or figuratively, as adolescents so often have done to make the transition to adulthood, he went "down to the sea in ships" with his father and found the wisdom and beauty of a new world that his father had found there. This, I think, is a wonderful metaphor of the possibilities, though it is somewhat tortured by the untimely death of Cousteau *fils* in the ocean depth.

It is intriguing, in any case, to contemplate how things might have been in human history if the state of affairs in the human psyche and spirit were such as to permit and prompt a different mythic story in Genesis 3. What if the story could have represented humanity as reaching forward within the will of God, reducing our generic and situational anxiety in life by deference toward each other, negotiation, and more generous evolution in relationships and goal achievement? What if we were not prone, instead, to revolution and violation? What if individuality, maturity, and wisdom, and our reach for knowledge of being like God in comprehending the world inside out, in knowing God as he now knows us, were managed patiently by nonviolent trial and error?

Today it takes therapy to help people to do that, and it always has. Cooperative growth with God and exploration of the possibilities of human destiny in tranquility is not a story that rings true to the human experience of dissonance, alienation, and dis-ease, but it suggests a redemptive alternative that might have been from the beginning. What if we were not so badly distorted by being born scared and remaining anxiety-laden throughout the complete birthing process which includes our process to adult maturity? The truth of the matter is the fact that we are not far enough advanced from the Chimpanzee to be capable of that. It seems apparent that the invitation of grace to move into the growth mode of that redemptive option is really the whole issue of God's grace and human health.

GOD'S IMAGE-BEARERS AND THE FALL

If we think of the fall story and of human dysfunction as destructive anxiety-reduction dynamics, a final significant question regarding human nature arises. In what sense do humans inherently reflect God's image (Gen 1:27) in choosing self-destructive or self-defeating courses of action?

The human behavior of will and ego over against power and authority reflects, and is possible because of, an essential dimension of God's nature in humans. We all possess the function and attribute of being independent creators and reflectively will-driven agents of our own destiny. In the story of the fall and in real human experience of pain, disorder, distortion, and dis-ease, humans act as independent creators, gone awry perhaps, and as agents choosing our own destinies, even if self-defeating at times. Those choices free humans to be persons and to grow, but they decrease the focus, efficiency, and gratification of that freedom and increase the dissonance, conflict, and erosive sense of alienation when they are less than optimal choices.

God, as independent agent, could also act in self-defeating ways, but apparently does not. That is a credit to God's moral character as an independent moral being, not a result of God's essential nature, as if God had no alternative. God chooses to act in a way that is true to himself. That reminds one of the cynic's joke. Can God create a rock that is so heavy that God cannot lift it? The joke has greatly entertained the superficial and cynical secularist and it has unduly troubled Christian philosophers. It is to the credit of superficial Christians and secular philosophers, perhaps, that it has troubled neither of them much, both thinking it quite absurd.

It is, however, a profound question. The answer is not the one that Christian philosophers have given, namely, that "God cannot create a rock too heavy for God to lift since that is out of keeping with God's true character, God's essence." The answer, I judge, is rather that God can very well create such a rock. God can do anything like that and any other sort of self-defeating thing, if he chooses to do so. Moreover, God can do it without ceasing to be God, contrary to the view of Christian philosophers. God would, of course, turn out to be a bad God in the moral sense of that term, as well as in its social sense. But God would not be a bad God in the ontological sense. God would still be God, and that is all that counts ontologically, that is, in the sense of God's existence. In that sense it is not different for God than for humans who can be bad morally and socially because they choose self-defeating behavior, but remain human in every ontological sense—in every sense of being.

The crucial issue is that God has not created a rock too heavy for God to lift, so to speak, and has not chosen to engage in any other self-defeating behavior because God has apparently chosen to behave with inviolate moral integrity. God has chosen to be true to his own nature and destiny. God is not merely locked into an inevitable moral quality because of his essence. God is free to choose, grow, explore, experiment, decide, and fail.

God has chosen not to do so; not because of his essence, but because of his moral integrity and therefore, all morality is ultimately a matter of aesthetics, because of God's aesthetic integrity and sensitivity that drive

God's decision against self-defeating behavior. That is a matter of appropriateness and proportion. God is trustworthy, not merely as a being defined by logic or ontological inevitability, but as a being who is psychologically committed to holiness. Yahweh is not the name of a Greek god in a pantheon of abstract qualities personified in archetypical figures. Yahweh is the name of the Hebrew God, who chooses, acts, could err as Jesus could have at the temptation, and who decides not to do so. Yahweh decides to be moral, gracious, and sensitive.

Humans image God in the integrity of their choice processes. In that we are independent choosers, creators, and producers of life, we image God and reflect his nature. We spoil the clear quality of that image when we choose to defeat ourselves in our growth endeavors or needs by inappropriate and disproportionate conduct that obstructs our true self-realization and self-actualization.

Such is the case in the fall story as the Hebrews understood it and edited it for inclusion in the Hebrew Bible. Such is the case in our daily failures to make sound, wholesome, and healing choices. Humans recapitulate the fall daily. That is undoubtedly why we so spontaneously perceive the authenticity of that ancient myth. Moreover, that is undoubtedly why God has embraced us all in unconditional and uncalculating grace: forgiveness for everybody, for everything, for evermore (Mic 7:18–20).

7

Modern Notions of Human Nature

INTRODUCTION

IT SEEMS INCREASINGLY CRUCIAL to our work in the helping professions to clarify the concepts of humanness prevalent in our culture and in our psychological theory and practice. We encounter daily numerous bizarre and destructive models of who and what humans are, in our clients, in our culture value system, and in ourselves. In that regard, it seems quite important to acknowledge that the development of the Western world was influenced by a number of anthropological traditions, but supremely that of St. Paul, in the New Testament.

Though Paul's idea of the nature of human beings is not always self-evident or easily ferreted out of the New Testament, he is the only New Testament theologian who developed anything approaching such a science. Paul himself was heavily influenced by three ancient traditions. His position stands in contrast to the Mesopotamian model. He absorbed or internalized the Greek and Hebrew traditions, though he struggled all his life to integrate them. Interestingly, he never succeeded at that. I wish in what follows to discuss at some length all three of those sources of Western anthropology, mediated through Paul, and attempt to suggest how we encounter and can deal with them in our time.

MESOPOTAMIAN ANTHROPOLOGY

The Mesopotamian concept of human nature was essentially a demeaning one. These ancient civilizations had a peculiar record of having developed a world view basically rooted in a monotheism and proliferated in a secondary polytheism. The Sumerians, Chaldeans, Babylonians, and Assyrians were not remarkably different from one another in this regard. Marduk was the Babylonian progenitor of all things and functioned in terms of a subordinate hierarchy of gods, who enhanced and/or complicated his enterprises.

In any case, all these civilizations derived from this theology a concept of man as a creature who was demeaned and dehumanized by being trapped in an arbitrary, unfriendly, divine order of things. The gods made man from the inferior earthly substance of clay and then gave him the divine destiny of being servant to the gods to supply their needs and deliver them from menial survival tasks. Humans were of earthly substance with heavenly achievement demands. Humanity was trapped by the very constituent nature of the gods as gods, and by the very inherent nature of the universe.

Because humans were innately inferior, they could never escape the predicament of their inferiority and their subservient role. In the face of that, the gods unreasonably demanded of humans a transcendent divine role and quality of achievement. Humans were provided only earthly resources but were held to divine requirements.

It was in terms of that enigma that the Mesopotamians tended to explain the problem of evil, suffering, and pain in human life. The problem of suffering, of sickness, and of human dysfunction derived from the monstrous nature of the gods and of the transcendent world imposed upon them. Humans held that the problem of psychological distortion in human nature was the consequence of that impasse, and the more stoic and optimistic of them suggested that the only way to salvation was by a combination of three things: vigorous hard work, a good streak of luck, and the endeavor to outsmart or outflank the gods. This is similar to the humorful irony of the Greek drama of Euripides.

The notion of pseudo-optimism, of course, was good only for poets and philosophers. Just as in the history of the Christian faith in a secular world, apologetics (rational defense of the faith) has functioned as an impressive, sophisticated enterprise, convincing only the apologists. Likewise in Mesopotamia, the poetic notion of an outside chance of human

Modern Notions of Human Nature

transcendence and survival was believable only for the poets. In the end, there was a sinister kind of pessimism like Hegel's. He held the optimistic notion of the progressive, upward evolution of history in which any movement or action tended to produce a reaction, out of the synthesis of which two forces, progress was forged.

Schopenhauer and Nietzsche saw a destructive determinism in Hegel's thought and concluded that it boxed humans into a fatal trap. Schopenhauer asked, "What about those poor fellows who are the victims of the conflict of forces in the war between Germany and France?" He and Nietzsche looked at Hegel's philosophy of magnificent progressive optimism and concluded, "The rub is that humans are trapped in that magnificent evolution and that is demeaning and pessimistic." They foresaw that it would eventually develop into the sadism of Hitler's final solution. So the Mesopotamian notion of the nature of humans was essentially demeaning and devaluing.

GREEK ANTHROPOLOGY

In contrast, the Greek notion of human nature was infinitely more secular and it was extremely optimistic. The Greek notion of humankind was a magnificent one. The Greeks went through an evolutionary process in which they dealt with this concept of anthropology in three different ways. If one had lived in the pre-Homeric times, in the second millennium BCE, one would have had the inclination periodically, at least if one had had the strength or the money, to go to the oracle of Delphi and inquire of the gods about one's destiny. We remember that Oedipus, the unwitting aspirant to the throne of Thebes, went there for that. The epic and dramatic literature of Homer, Hesiod, Aeschylus, Sophocles and Euripides repeatedly recount the stories of their contemporaries and the Greek ancients traveling to Delphi to inquire of the gods about the outcome of a battle, their strategy in waging war, or some other facet of their destiny. Plato's dialogues and Socrates' reported discourses imply that it was a natural thing to inquire of Apollo at his oracle at Delphi.

When one went to the Delphic oracle, one entered the portals of the temple under an inscription that said, "Know thyself!" Hans Dieter Betz points out that in pre-Homeric times that meant, "Remember, you are just a mortal! When you go through these gates, be sure that you confess your status by saying to Apollo, 'Thou art!'" So there was a dialogue implied in the superscription. The pilgrim said, "O Apollo, thou art!" and Apollo said, "Know thyself. Remember you are merely mortal." Betz points out that merely mortal meant the same thing as "to err is human." That was a confronting experience for the Greek, but as is true of honest confrontation with oneself and with the gods, it had in it the seeds of health.

The Greek who confronted himself in terms of the primitive meaning of Delphi was already coming to grips with his mere humanness, coming to grips with the fact that he was indeed the kind of creature in which it was native and natural to err. That sounds demeaning, but the implication is magnificent. As psychological healers and Christians we should understand that better than anyone, knowing that if we come honestly to grips with our realities we are already a long way down the road to managing them constructively. Fortunately that is what happened for the Greeks. It was the "universal education" impact of that primitive anthropology, mediated into the Greek cultural and psychological process by the oracle at Delphi, that produced the surprising humanist experience that the Greeks achieved.

That first stage of Greek anthropology prevailed from that point on through the epic era of Homer to the Ionian scientific age of the sixth century BCE and the golden age of Pericles. Five hundred years before Christ, when Socrates reigned in his creative humanist thought, there developed a progressive metamorphosis in which the second stage of the Greek notion of human nature arose. For Socrates and others who contemplated the superscription at Delphi, "Know thyself" had come to mean not only, "remember your mere humanness" but also, "accept your humanness compassionately and joyfully, not despairingly."

To be merely human was one thing. To be compassionately human was quite a new thing. It was a transcendent step admirably beyond the primitive insight of honest self-acceptance. The Greeks discovered that the more they thought about that, the more significant humans seemed and the less significant the gods seemed. Greek theology began with a kind of animistic notion of god infesting every facet of nature. It was a primitive attempt to explain the mysterious powers present in the cosmos. That metamorphosed to the point where gods were given names, personalities, and domains. Poseidon was the god of the sea, for example. The problem of gods and power and threats in nature was lifted from animism to polytheism. So it was not just a matter of encountering an indefinable spiritual power when a mysterious wave suddenly sprang up out of the sea and overturned your boat and destroyed your goods or your family. Now you could identify the god of that particular domain that threatened you and you had his name and could manipulate him. You could make a sacrifice to Poseidon to placate him and that gave you some power to manage him. Once you gave him a name and a biography you could predict his behavior, to a certain extent, and thus exercise some reasonable power with regard to him. You could develop liturgies and rituals to influence him in your favor before you left the Athenian harbor of Piraeus for the Peloponnesus.

While the Hebrew and Greek anthropology are remarkably different from their Mesopotamian precursors, they are also remarkably different from each other. The Greek notion of human nature seems to have evolved from primitive and demeaning anxiety about the fragile humanness, to the admirable confidence of Socratic Humanism. Apparently, the Dorian migrants pulled themselves upward from the status of victims of the vagaries of nature to the masters of land and sea. They moved psychologically and culturally from nomadic hunters to domesticated farmers, and on to civilized urbanites. Their dynamic struggle was to replace their fear of the mysterious spirit-filled unknown in nature with the identifiable gods whose personalities could be described and whose behavior could be both predicted and managed. Then they struggled to replace these increasingly manageable gods with demi-god like men and finally with real humans themselves, in charge of their own destiny. They became secure in unmystified rationality.

As the gods became more tame they became more laughable. As they became more laughable they became less necessary. The roles of a godlike and Christ-like Prometheus, or a Herakles who civilizes society by brute force, and a Jason who civilizes human culture by humane means, are intriguing and wonderful. These help us in our endeavor to understand and appreciate the evolution of the Greek anthropology. Tracing the process in which the awesome gods became humorous, the humorous gods laughable, and the laughable gods scandalous and irrelevant is itself a surprisingly hilarious enterprise. Equally awesome and profoundly sobering is the visualization of how fragile and demeaned humans became vigorous, clever, and durable. Humans became honorable, estimable, and heroic. Humans, in the Greek experiment, became more moral than the gods, more humane than their creators, more masterful than the incredible, preoccupied and irrelevant population of Olympus. That magnificent metamorphosis was the miracle of Greece.

Zeus, for example, was repeatedly pictured in venal pursuits unbecoming of the heroic and virtuous. He was perpetually chasing young maidens around the countryside, with his wife, Hera, scolding, maligning, and berating him. The gods first became identifiable, then manageable, then laughable, and finally irrelevant, as I said above. As the gods became irrelevant, humans became increasingly significant. The significance lay in the fact that humans began to see themselves, not as merely human, but as compassionately and transcendently human. The Greeks came to the conclusion that it is not only true that "to err is human," but that "to forgive is human." There is about human beings that potential for compassion that is ultimately redeeming in our own view, the Greeks discovered.

Finally, the golden age of Greek humanism arrived, with the Greeks achieving the notion that humans were not just compassionately human. Humanity was magnificently human. So magnificently human was humanity, they concluded, that the whole of human destiny was in human hands. The slogan of the golden age was "Mankind is the measure of all things." "Know thyself" had come to mean, "realize, affirm, and actualize your true magnificence."

In that process, of course, the Greeks had to deal also with the problem of evil, or failure and dysfunction. They dealt with the problem in nature and the universe by saying that the problems of pain and suffering were only apparent. "What we used to think were the whims of the gods afflicting us out of avarice, insensitivity, or ignorance, are really only the normal and natural processes of nature. The only real evil is in man's inhumanity to man." That is not a force of evil out there. It is a correctable behavior devolving from human choices.

The Greeks endeavored to manage that in the humanistic age by identifying the two sides of human nature: magnificent human rationality and unfortunate human animality. These constituted the magnificent and the malignant in human behavior, for the Greeks. These represented the contest between the mind and the body, the *psyche* and the *sarx*, the spiritual and the fleshly or carnal. The destiny of rational man was, therefore, seen as the responsibility to subject the sarx to the dominion of the psyche, to place the flesh under the control of the mind and spirit, human rationality. The primacy of the intellect and the implied triumph of the spirit over the flesh, the higher passions over the lower ones, was finally conceived by the Greeks as the road to salvation.

Modern Notions of Human Nature

The centuries that followed the golden age, of course, tell and interesting story of despair and disillusion. Humanity as divine proved impossible for humans to manage. Humanity finally did not measure up to the "godness" or even the "goodness" they assigned to themselves. Existentialist loss of meaning set in and brought on a wholesale lunge into primitive mystery religions, the philosophies of the Cynics, Stoics, Epicureans, and numerous others in the search for stable meaning, and then the bizarre supernaturalism that followed. The unfortunate course is similar to the pattern of history from the humanism of the nineteenth-century Western rationalism to the existentialist despair of Camus, Sartre, Kierkegaard, and Schopenhauer at the turn of the century. This has issued forth into the present day preoccupation with astrology, karma, reincarnation, and numerous other experiments in the meaning quest in the West.

HEBREW ANTHROPOLOGY

The third significant anthropological tradition in the ancient world that fed Paul's concept of human nature is the Hebrew one. It is a subtle, simple, majestic tradition. It is essentially the story of humankind in the Old Testament. In very brief summary it is the story of Yahweh, the covenanting God, embracing humans unconditionally as sons and daughters of God.

The story of the nature of human beings in Hebrew thought may be looked at from various directions. First, it is a unitary notion throughout. The Hebrew anthropology knows nothing of the division of body, mind, and spirit, so prominent in the Greek model. It knows nothing of the tension or contrast the Greeks saw between flesh and spirit, *sarx* and *psyche*. For the Hebrews humans beings are one and unified. It is not so much the body that requires redirection or suppression; it is not so much a matter of the dominance of *soma* or *sarx* by *psyche*. It is out of the heart that the issues of life flow, namely, out of the center of ones' being, one's self. Humans are persons to the Hebrews, persons and personalities, and must be dealt with as totalities.

This was so true for the Hebrews that they had a great deal of difficulty conceptualizing death. There is no reference in the Old Testament to a specific experience of a soul going to heaven at death, or going to hell. The Hebrews continued to talk about death and Sheol as an undifferentiated and undefined state. Sheol was the equivalent in Hebrew as the underworld was for the other cultures around the Middle East at that time, but not as specifically conceptualized. One died and entered into a different kind of existence, but the concept of differentiation was not complete. One reason was that they had difficulty dealing with the notion that a person could be split; that when the body is dead there is something else that goes somewhere else. They thought of persons as one. The unitary concept of the person is the first essential principle in the Hebrew notion of human nature.

The second element in Hebrew anthropology, detailed in a previous chapter, is the concept of the co-regent or co-worker with God in God's world. That is a majestic notion of a human's nature and role that stands in contrast with the human predicament in the world of secularity. The Greeks had to get rid of the gods in order for humans to fully come into their own. The Mesopotamians could never gain that transcendent humanness and had to trick the gods in order to achieve any kind of freedom or control of their own destiny. For the Hebrews, humans became fully human in close covenantal relationship with God in which God and humans were abjectly, unconditionally, uncalculatingly, and eternally committed to each other. The Hebrews thought of human beings as made in the image of God, genitals and all. There was no reason to perceive a moral disjunction between the lower and higher passions. All human needs, expressions, and activities reflected some aspect of God's nature. Humans could relate, imagine, create, love, communicate, produce life, and build things, just like God can do.

Paul picks up the Hebrew notion of man and deals with it in three terms. He speaks, in effect, of what might be called primordial humanity: humanity in the pristine state of conformity to God's primeval design. He speaks secondly of fallen man, as depicted in Romans 1–5, where the contrast is boldly focused between God's design for humans and what humans end up being. Finally he speaks of the man in Christ. It seems clear that when Paul said he was a Hebrew of the Hebrews, one of the things definitely implied is his heavy dependence on this Semitic Hebrew anthropological model and tradition. Fortunately, or perhaps unfortunately, for Paul and his own peace of mind and psycho-intellectual integration, he was caught up in a world where he found himself dealing with a significant tension between the humanist notion of humanity from the Greek anthropological mainstream and the theistic notion of humans from the Hebrew mainstream.

Paul was not toying with humanism, although from a certain perspective his anthropology might be described as a Christian humanism. He was trying to integrate the unitary notion of humanity and the Greek notion of

Modern Notions of Human Nature

humanity, which were at war within him: *soma/sarx* and *psyche*, the lower and higher passions. "The good that I would, I do not. The evil that I would not, that I do. Who will deliver me from this continual deadliness."

Ridderbos (1997, *Paul, An Outline of His Theology*) deals with the problem of soma, sarx, and psyche in Paul and points out that the apostle ends up with a Christian anthropology in which the Hebrew and Greek traditions are reasonably and adequately integrated. There remains, however, a tension, which comes out in the following manner as regards our concern as Christian counselors.

Paul consistently wishes to say that primordial humans, in the face of the predicament of fallen humanity, always exist as a kind of ideal. Salvation comes, nevertheless, only when we transcend both the pristine state of Eden and the state of our brokenness, alienation, fallenness, and pathology, and become persons in Christ. What does that mean? It means for persons, always in the context of the community of faith, to experience the relief of Christ's grace: to be in the way of Christ's mode of life, and in a certain sense to incarnate the character of Christ, to be in the Body of Christ—the Church spiritually conceived. It means for a human to be one in whom Christ can be seen to function.

However, while trying to hold firmly to that, on the one hand, Paul deals with the problem of the disorder in human nature in terms of the Greek categories: flesh and spirit. "There is a war within me," he says. It is a tension between the psyche and the soma/sarx. That tension Paul sometimes tends to resolve as the Greeks did: the management and suppression of the flesh by the dominance by the mind, rationality, or spirit. Clearly it was a problem for Paul to work out.

In the end Paul is really sure that the only salvation is in Christ's deliverance of him from the entire perplexity. That deliverance is a gift. It is unconditional. It is free and unmerited. At the same time, there is a discipline implied in that gift of grace. The discipline implied is the management of the lower passions by the higher, a strictly and bold-faced Greek idea.

CONTEMPORARY CULTURE

We are dealing in our world with essentially four anthropologies that function in our cultural, social, and psychological processes. We see it in ourselves and in our patients or clients, and congregations; in our own minds, in the minds of our colleagues, both Christian and secular, and in the minds of those we serve and endeavor to heal. Undoubtedly this latter is even a more crucial factor in these four models that shape our lives.

One of these anthropological models prominent right now in our culture is the Mesopotamian—that devastating and demeaning notion of human beings as trapped. It seems to me that Schopenhauer can be thanked for that. Hegel conceived of the whole of the human experiment in a very optimistic way, saying that history is the interplay of thesis, antithesis, and synthesis; and as a consequence of that dynamic, history is moving progressively both forward and upward to the ideal society—the kingdom or reign of God. Schopenhauer perceived that the problem with Hegel's model was that "humans are trapped."

Humanity is trapped. The existentialism of Camus and Sartre which dominated French thought during the Great Depression and World War II poured into American culture through our universities after the war and bore its nihilist fruit in the cultural revolution of the 1960s, 70s, and 80s. Their general philosophical tone and temper has permeated and pervaded the last half of the twentieth century. It continues now in the twenty-first century. It has trapped the spirits of many of our patients and fellow citizens. It is really the Mesopotamian anthropology: the demeaning despair of the trapped human, the helpless, hopeless, depressed cynic, who turns to drink, drugs, or terrorism with increasing urgency.

The second prevalent model of humankind is the notion of the Greeks. That is the incredible optimism of the secular human who is the measure of all things, whose destiny is in his or her own hands. Such are the persons who feel free to wreck the middle class to gain the power and resources to become filthy rich, with only their own destiny in view. Today some women feel free to do anything with their own bodies with no moral sense that there are others who have a rightful interest in what they do, particularly the non-voting child which they readily abort as though it were toilet waste, another kind of unwanted excrement from their bloated system. These folk seem to believe that all they need to do is get a sufficient education, preferably at public expense, gain sufficient insight, develop sufficient rationality, or receive psychoanalysis or psychotherapy; and they are saved for themselves and their creative exploitive destiny at other's expense.

There is also a less malignant form of this model in which the ideals of individual humanism seem to be the motivational ideal of many persons. They generally are less unlawful than the Enron criminals and the morally promiscuous. There is something wonderfully entertaining and attractive about this model of sheer self-actualization and self-realization, without thought of others. I could very easily be a humanist. I could quite easily be a secular humanist. I like the idea of being a Christian humanist. That means I am always tempted, as are we all, with this second model of human nature which goes for the gold, so to speak, and leaves everyone else to make his or her own way as well. Ayn Rand's *Virtue of Selfishness* (1964), is a marvelous book, very close to Christian ethics, in which she argues that if we do not seek our own interests with vigor, and exclusive focus, we will never be the best we can be for the rest of society.

The third model of humankind is a secularized Hebrew notion, the concept of human beings as unitary phenomena, who have all the prerogatives and possibilities of their own meanings and destinies written into the structure of their individuality. This is a hybrid of the idea of humans as magnificently pre-programmed by genetic design, on the one hand, and the radical notion of the virtue of selfishness, on the other. To be healthy and human means to be more totally and authentically individual and thus be more wholesome for everybody. As I noted, Ayn Rand is the champion of this notion. She suggests that the whole notion of Christian sacrificial or other-oriented love and care, agape, is really a subterfuge. If you really want to be wholesome for the world, you must cultivate creative selfishness. If you are really good for yourself, then you are really best for everybody else. The idea of genetic pre-programmed humans is reinforced by the influence upon anthropology of the new inquiry into the DNA chain and the possibilities of genetic management or manipulation. There is something so close to the truth about both facets of this model that it really is a subtle and tempting possibility. Both notions have a significant dimension of truth in them.

The fourth anthropology is the Christian model. I do not agree totally with Ridderbos that Paul successfully integrated the Greek and Hebrew anthropologies and formulated a thoroughgoing Christian anthropology. I am much more inclined to feel that Paul might profitably have stayed closer to the Hebrew Yahwist model of human nature. The Christian concept of human nature has at least these dimensions. First, it requires that we take our human predicament seriously, namely that we acknowledge that the problem of humans is a radical problem. The problem of our disorder, of our disorientation, our brokenness, our alienation, our proclivity to lose the sense of the meaningfulness of things, cuts right through to the center of our existence—our being itself. In the final analysis, our problem is, not how many sins we have committed but who we know ourselves to be. It is a problem of identity and character. While the fall story was written as a way of taking account of this brokenness, it is probably closer to the truth that our problem is that we are not far enough, as yet, from the Chimpanzee.

A Christian concept of human nature is the concept of persons who are fundamentally disordered but possessing two crucial redemptive potentials. The first one, prominent in the Hebrew notion, is the native, healthy integrating urge of life itself to health, to wholesomeness, to what we are designed by God to be. The second is the possibility in Christ to become not only a compatriot of God, but a healer in God's world, through the experience of God's gracious acceptance. That is, we can become the incarnation of Christ in the present moment. We can be the Body of Christ. In that sense, we can be Christ for others, not just compatriots of God, but God in Christ present through us for our fractured world.

We encounter all these models and their consequences continually in our interaction with clients. If we fail to clarify the model of humans in these terms, we tend to lose efficiency in achieving healing. One of the great disorders we constantly encounter and should recognize is the disorder of identity. Some of the worst human suffering is observed in the person who cannot conceive of himself or herself as one who is beloved, who can be the potential object of graciousness. Yet that is the fundamental element in the Christian concept of human nature.

In Jesus, grace meant unconditionally accepting the adulterous woman, ordaining the denying Peter, embracing Judas and addressing him in the garden of Gethsemane as "Friend." So when Jesus said, "As the Father sent me into the world, so send I you," he must have meant that we should deal in the Christian notion of humanity, namely, as purveyors and potential receivers of that experience of grace. On the Mount of Olives his last words to his disciples were, "You shall be exhibits (*marturian*) of me in the court room of world opinion" (Acts1).

8

Consequences for Psychotherapy

JOHANN VON GOETHE OBSERVED that everybody wants to be somebody but nobody wants to grow. That is not a universally applicable fact of life, but unfortunately it is what the therapist often confronts in the clinic. That is, healing, education, maturation, spiritual growth, and redemption take time, require work, and are a process of development. There is a profound sense in which illness, ignorance, immaturity, and irreligion are states or postures produced by obstruction of the growth we all need. Moreover, the states of wholeness, wisdom, knowledge, maturity, wholesomeness, and salvation are the integrated achievements to which growth brings us.

The process of growth hinges upon insight and the application of insight to our illness or need and to the possibilities and methods for inciting growth toward healing. This is true and can be applied to all aspects of our need, whether what obstructs our health is psychological, physiological, intellectual, theological, spiritual, or a combination of these.

This insight is most healing when it is developed in the light of a Christian anthropology, structured by a Yahwist theology of grace: unconditional, radical, and universal, as I have articulated in previous chapters. That is, I believe that God has imputed to us an inviolable status of God-compatriot. We are not merely God's servants or children. We have a status and role of being co-laborers with God in the "garden" of his Kingdom, God's reign in the human world. We are companions of God in that communion that is idealized by Adam's walks with God in the cool of the evening. We are imagers of God's essential qualities or characteristics of communication, creativity, generativity, memory, self-awareness, self-consciousness, decisiveness, power, self-actualization, love, and the like. This assumption or faith position, moreover, includes the perception that not even God will abrogate that status, and that therefore God cannot.

This Christian anthropology implies that the nature of humans is being shaped by a discernable spectrum of magnificent potentials for psychological, physical, intellectual, and spiritual growth. These, in turn, have remarkable potential for technological, scientific, cultural, and religious growth. This Christian anthropology further conceives the destiny of humans as the achievement of wholeness and integration through total actualization of the potentials inherent in humanness, namely inherent in the status of God-compatriot and the bearer of the image of God.

A PSYCHOTHEOLOGY OF HEALTH

Thus, viewed psychologically or theologically, a complete understanding of humans is grounded in that dimension of anthropology having to do with the chief purpose of our existence. We are all called to a special destiny to which we are inevitably coming by the grace of God. Our destiny is shaped by what we can be and what we are designed to be. Christian anthropology is teleological in orientation. That means that our destiny is shaped by its intended outcome. Viewed psychologically or theologically, wholeness is the destiny or the outcome of our growth and maturation. That may well be true of the entire cosmos, as well. In that case, health is the state of having achieved wholeness, or being in the process of achieving it, in the degree appropriate to our stage of growth and place in the universe at any given time.

Christian psychologists, theologians, and clinicians, therefore, must work with clinical criteria for assessing the process and a person's stage in it. Secular psychology, insofar as it represents authentic insight and scientific truth regarding that level of the process that it has investigated, provides Christians with much ready-made equipment and insight for this endeavor. That secular equipment and insight must be received gratefully and seriously, as a gift from God, and then employed in a psychotheological framework.

The dynamics of health and wholeness described above apply equally to physiological, psychological, intellectual, and spiritual spheres. They are equally true with regard to sickness of body, mind, and spirit. They apply as much to clinical psychopathology as to spiritual or religious disorder.

Consequences for Psychotherapy

A PSYCHOTHEOLOGY OF ILLNESS

If things make sense thus far, we can attempt to define or describe a psychotheology of illness. In general the subconscious feeling in professionals and laypersons alike, regarding people who are ill, is surprisingly negative and stereotyped. The attitude of our culture is often that they are sick because they did not exercise enough, diet effectively, eat well enough, protect themselves properly, live well, stay youthful, or choose parents with good genetics. We spontaneously assume that they are ill because God, fate, aging, destiny, or their misbehavior has finally caught up with them. We must admit that the ill are seen as second-class citizens. They are exploited, objectified, warehoused, manipulated, and generally handled as many preachers handle sinners. Something in us arrogantly infers that the ill are getting what is coming to them, though we may empathize or sympathize.

That psychotheology of illness will not square with our Christian anthropology and the theology of grace. A sound psychotheology of illness must operate from the perspective that ill persons are God-compatriots of infinitely and inviolably worthy status. Their growth toward their divinely destined self-actualization at the physical, psychological, intellectual, or spiritual level has been obstructed. That state of obstruction and the loss of growth appropriate to the person's current level of expected development is by definition illness.

Sometimes the obstruction is a genetic distortion, a foreign organism, an imbalance of nutrition, a dysfunction of metabolism, or a serious organ failure. It can be a disrupted social life, inappropriate or neurotic fear, a failure of appropriate instruction and guidance, spiritually unsatisfying worship, unchanneled assertiveness, or some other psychological deficiency.

Whatever it proves to be, insight in the patient or applied by the healer is necessary to free the suffering person for growth toward health and wholeness once again. Illness is not a state that implies moral failure, but an existential state of affairs concerning which the only moral issue is whether the healer and the patient promote healing if and where it is potentially available.

A PSYCHOTHEOLOGY OF HEALING

It is predictable, therefore, that a psychotheology of healing deals with the method and substance of the work of reducing obstructions to growth and enhancing its vitality. This is the immediate level of concern of the clinician. It is imperative that the clinician's model of humanness is shaped by a dynamic Christian anthropology, structured in terms of a theology of grace. This enables the psychotheology of illness, healing, and health or wholeness to be a sound one. Moreover, the clinician's Christian anthropology must be dynamic and not static or dogmatic. It must be interacting constantly with his or her real clinical experience. This is true for any Christian scientific researcher. Interaction is crucial between the clinical level, the data base level, research methodology level, and theoretical or theory development level. Thus the clinician's Christian anthropology is constantly being reshaped and refined by the combined experience of all four levels of the quest, and thus progressively maturing.

MODELS OF PSYCHOPATHOLOGY AND PSYCHOTHERAPY

In 1974 Siegler and Osmond provided some interesting insights and a useful focus for the field of clinical psychology. In *Models of Madness, Models of Medicine*, they presented a table of eight current models of psychopathology. For each model they described twelve typical clinical functions, including diagnosis or definition, etiology, subject behavior, treatment, prognosis, therapy setting, types of therapists, rights of the patient and of the patient's social unit, and the goals of the therapy. The *DSM V* reflects some of these aspects (2015).

The Siegler and Osmond current models are defined as follows. The *medical model* assumes a physician will diagnose the illness, rule out other diagnoses, inform the patient, and determine treatment and prognosis. Natural causes are assumed to be the sources of the disorder. The goal of the process is to prevent worsened illness, to cure the symptoms and, if possible the disease, and to accumulate medical knowledge.

The *moral model* assumes that a moral practitioner or ethicist will determine the nature and extent of the dysfunction or inappropriate and hence immoral behavior. The etiology is assumed to be unimportant but is learned bad behavior. Treatment modifies the bad behavior with discipline: positive and negative sanctions. Prognosis is considered good if the patient cooperates in the establishing of functional sanction systems and reinforcement schedules. The goal of therapy is to alter the patient's a-social or anti-social behavior with acceptable social norms.

Consequences for Psychotherapy

The *impaired model* sees the patient as permanently maimed and unconcerned with most of the twelve functions, except diagnosis and institutionalization. The goal is to protect the patient from society and *vice versa*. Anything short of permanent impairment is not identified as clinical pathology.

The *psychoanalytic model* assumes patients are somewhere on a continuum from mild neurosis to severe psychosis. Diagnosis is not significant, etiology is very important, therapy involves decoding the patient's symbolic systems and creating the transference base that will enhance the patent's move toward health. The patient has the right to sympathy, empathy, and progress toward health. The goal is to resolve the pathogenic conflicts, intrapsychic or psychosocial in nature.

The *social model* assumes that society is sick and the patient's pathology is accidental to that. The sociopathology of the patient can be corrected by social change in the community environment. The rights and goals of society, the patient, and the therapist focus on creation of a healthy social environment for growth, especially in children.

The *psychedelic model* sees psychopathology as a mind-expanding trip prompted by families or communities who drive patients crazy. Therapy involves breaking the family bond, providing a "guided trip" to enlightenment, and so allowing the patient to develop the inner potential to change his or her self and world.

The *conspirational model* assumes that pathology is a label given to patients by others who cannot tolerate deviance. Treatment is brainwashing for the purpose of maintaining the *status quo*.

The *family interactional model* assumes that patients are the index of the family's pathology. Family therapy is required and, if effective, the family will give up its pathological game pattern and the index person can drop the personal symptoms. The goal of therapy is to understand the family dynamics and restore pathological families to functional relationships.

It is evident that each of the models described comprehends some aspects of the truth with which clinicians must deal. It is interesting that the theorist who has come closest to devising a psychotheology of illness and therapy, Jay Adams, falls into the moral model. His work is least reflective of the full range of data available and the farthest from sound psychology and psychotherapy. He has no Christian anthropology rooted in a thoroughgoing theology of grace, in the biblical tradition of the Yahwist.

It is impossible here to critique each of the Sieglar-Ormond categories in detail, but a few observations may be useful. First, the social model, though it embodies some reality, has proven thoroughly dysfunctional in our society, as indicated by the hopeless ineffectiveness of the costly strategies for basic social change attempted over the last half century by individual, communal, or federal initiatives. It is indicated further by the recent acknowledgement that the longstanding ambition for criminal rehabilitation has not worked and is scientifically and culturally bankrupt. It is interesting that the only exception to this failure seems to be the federal program for rehabilitation of sex offenders.

The impaired model and conspiratorial model offer little comprehensive usefulness at all. The psychedelic model is a new research and experimental model in the form of clinical human trials of a very specific and controlled nature. The early results seem to suggest that there might be a resurgence of the psychedelic model as an additional resource within the medical model. The medical model and the family interaction model are much more comprehensively applicable. Both are deficient, however, in their assessment of the seriousness of the patient's depth and degree of disorder.

The psychoanalytic model comes closest to appreciating the radical extent and depth of human dysfunction and the alienation from our real human potentials for self-actualization and our grand human destiny in God's grace. Like the medical and family interaction models, it fails to appreciate adequately the pathological state of human beings generally, and the rather high percentage of people who are suffering from some degree of psychological distress. It fails to appreciate the real dimension of generalized pathogenic anxiety and dissonance, intrapsychic and psychosocial, which lie at the root of human pathology, and are inherent in the current state of humanness. The self-perceived fallenness, brokenness, alienation and isolation (lostness) at the core of our humanness is generally underestimated.

A CHRISTIAN CLINICAL APPROACH

A Christian psychotheological model of pathology and therapy is essential for preceding wisely in our field. It must include an adequate appreciation of our real sense of universal human brokenness and lostness, expressive of the distance between our destiny and our daily function. That means we need to discern the distance between our potentials and our problematic

Consequences for Psychotherapy

state of underachievement, and between our creative imagination and our performance. We are able to idealize a perfect world. We have the ability to created only a flawed one. In sum, it is a matter of the distance between our reach and our grasp.

In a previous chapter, I noted that in developing psychological theory, the history of personality theory could be categorized in four different models: those theories assuming human personality to be essentially rational, emotional, relational, or biological. A brief discussion of these four models is relevant to the development of a sound Christian clinical perspective.

If one assumes, as Socrates did and Albert Ellis did, that human nature or personality is essentially rational, then pathology is the lack or loss of "the well-considered life." This suggests that intellectual wholeness comes by information through education. Psychological wholeness then comes by insight through informative therapy, being led to think rightly. Spiritual wholeness is then dependent upon comprehension of the wisdom of God in Christ, generally considered to be dogmatic in form and propositional in expression. The lack of insight and information at any of these levels produces pathology in that category of human function affected by the lack, according to rational types of personality theory.

If one assumes that human nature is essentially emotional, as Maslow and Rogers have thought, then true humanness is achieved in authentic emotionality. Implied in this set of personality theories is the notion that pathology is the obstruction or lack of authenticity and freedom of the emotional fields or emotional world of the person. This does not imply that emotions are always arbitrarily productive or affirmable, or that it is always more healthy to act on any or all emotions at any or all times It implies rather that the potential to do so, and the freedom to decide about that, is crucial to authentic humanness and health.

In this model, intellectual health is achieved by freeing the emotive world through training to offer its truth and reality to the cognitive perception of things. Psychological health requires that emotional freedom that eliminates intrapsychic dissonance or confliction. This will lead to psychosocial adjustment, coping, and health. The lack of that freedom is pathological and pathogenic, that is, it is sick and creates mental illness.

The relational model assumes that persons achieve selfhood and wholeness only in and by relationality. This is different than saying good emotional or rational relationships produce health. It is rather the assertion that we are authentic and complete selves only while interacting. Gestalt and EST might be cited as cases in point. Pathology results from the fear or lack of opportunity to interact, to confront and assert one's self with or over against another person. Health at each level is the function of actual encounter and the change it induces in the state of being of the person while encountering. Some residual effect is assumed, but it is not valued except as it is realized in the next encounter.

The biological model with its Skinnerian determinism assumes that pathology is the breakdown of response to stimuli, and health is the restoration of efficient stimulus-response process. Behaviorism provides useful insights, but seems to me that its real value is grossly disproportionate to its current popularity and press.

Christian clinicians need to use the insights from all four categories in building a clinically functional Christian anthropology and psychotheology. However, the one that lends itself most readily to the clinical perspective rooted in a sound and thoroughgoing theology of grace is the emotional model. It takes the entire question of the human spirit, human nature as a divine image, human potential, and personal self-actualization very seriously. Moreover, it has the potential of deeply honoring the fragile human longing for a grace-like, unconditional personal regard.

Rogers' notion of the inviolable integrity of the person and personality of the patient at the point where he or she is in any given therapeutic moment or event, lends itself to the grace-oriented clinical perspective. Rogers' process model of psychotherapy and his concept of the fully functioning person as the goal of therapy and of life, provide a useful framework for Christian clinical work. That kind of approach is amenable to embracing the function of a Hebrew type of perception of truth and reality while valuing no less the historic Western emphasis on the Greek type of scientific methodology.

The development of the Christian therapeutic strategy that adequately reflects the kind of Christian anthropology that is implied in a thoroughgoing grace theology will include the following applied characteristics. First, the incarnation in the therapist of his or her unconditional acceptance of the patient, where the patient is at the moment in his or her pathology.

Second, a profound empathy that places the therapist inside the psychological frame of reference in which the patient experiences the pathology. This will lead to the therapist's endeavor to determine the sources and nature of the obstructions to health as well as the possibilities, in and for the patient, for reinitiating growth. This empathic incarnation of God's grace

Consequences for Psychotherapy

empowers the therapist to affirm the patient as a person, not just as patient, as God affirms us in taking us and our alienation so seriously as to visit us in his son. Such verbal and nonverbal mediation of God's unconditional acceptance of persons, including the patient, is a crucial baseline for the patient's recovery of a perception of self-worth, empowerment, and destiny that rings true to his or her real nature as a potentially whole person—God's whole person. It can give the patient the experience of being fulfilled in all the possibilities that are arbitrarily imputed to him or her as a compatriot of God in the work of his world, and as a person who is created in God's image.

Third, the Christian therapist will provide the patient with a sense of the mutuality of the quest for wholeness for the patient, upon which the patient-therapist team has embarked. Fourth, it will be made evident in the therapy process that the therapist, too, is wrestling with his or her own humanness, with both its pathology and its potential. Fifth, it will become evident in a sound Christian therapeutic strategy that the therapist's world view expresses a comprehensive ambition for the wholeness of the whole world of humans and things, and that the patient's wholeness is quested for in that setting or context.

Sixth, the possibilities and expectations for the patient's wholeness inherent in that worldview will become apparent. Seventh, the grace-imputed status of the patient as compatriot of God will become evident to the patient, as the underpinning reality of the worldview. Eighth, soundly established techniques for countering defensive patterns in the patient will be utilized to defeat any obstruction of growth to wholeness.

Ninth, the patient's physical, intellectual, psychological, and spiritual needs and states will be taken seriously as functions of a whole-person concern for wholeness and wholesomeness. Tenth, the effectiveness of therapy will be measured in relative terms at each level of increased functionality—physical, psychological, intellectual, and spiritual—in the light of the expectation that the ultimate achievement of health will be the arrival at spiritual, as well as psychological, maturity.

Some Christian professionals, active especially in pastoral care movements, have severely denigrated the clinical perspective and psycho-theological model of healing. They are reverting to what Wayne Oates (*Pastoral Counseling*, 1974) has called a pseudo-classical style of pastoral counseling. Evangelicalism and fundamentalist pastors have tended in this direction ever since Freud brought out his key works. They have largely missed the development of psychodynamic psychology superseding Freud's psychoanalytic theory. They have not noticed the strong movement of modern pastoral counseling as represented by such professional training organizations as Clinical Pastoral Supervision and Psychotherapy, Clinical Pastoral Education, and the American Association for Pastoral Counseling, to say nothing about modern modes of psychotherapy.

The fundamentalist perspective tends to be moralistic rather than psychodynamic and grace oriented. This erroneous attempt to relate Christian faith and the healing enterprise is a morally forced imposition upon the patient rather than standing with the patient in the pathology with the tools of help and health. That approach cannot be of any service to the Christian concern and dialogue for authentic psychotheology. It is a return to a directive form of imposed church authority upon the helping professions instead of a modern model of Christian healing. It undermines the progress we have made during the last four or five decades in Christian psychotherapy. That regression is to be assiduously avoided. Both psychology and theology have managed too well and come too far to warrant an anti-clinical and anti-grace-theology iconoclasm at this point.

CLINICAL CONSEQUENCES FOR PSYCHOTHERAPY

The consequences for psychotherapy of a thoroughgoing grace theology and the Christian anthropology inherent in it might be elaborated at great length. I have done that in other publications (*Radical Grace*, 2007). Here I shall merely summarize the more obviously relevant effects.

To operate clinically from the perspective that humans image God and are imputed an inviolable status of God-compatriot, leads the therapist first of all to an appreciation of human persons as of infinite worth, dignity, and esteem, and as possessing a pre-established identity to be fully realized through growth and insight, in spite of themselves and untrammeled by their illness. Second, it urges upon the therapist the principle that the root of pathology is alienation, requiring eclipse by a God-like acceptance of the patient by the therapist, as agent of God's healing intention.

Third, it urges that the acceptance is unconditional. This perspective will include the perception on the part of the therapist and the patient that they are both pathological pilgrims on a journey together. Fourth, it urges that sin is more precisely a failure of destiny than a failure of duty, and therefore is better designated as our sickness than as our moral failure.

Consequences for Psychotherapy

Fifth, the goal of therapy and the view of the possibilities of wholeness in the patient are greatly clarified by this perspective I have urged. Sixth, the above insights will work toward defusing neurotic guilt, anxiety, remorse, hopelessness, grief, self-pity, low self-esteem, and compulsivity; and will restore a sense of inherent dignity and freedom in the patient.

Seventh, this clinical model is likely to remove the panic of the therapist regarding the awesome clinical responsibility to bring health to the patient. This frees the therapist to make the God-like decisions often necessary in therapeutic process. This clinical model should also effect meaningful, constructive anxiety-reduction for the patient who perceives that he or she does not need to get well in order to be accepted and cherished, certified and honored, by the therapist or by God. Thus the patient is free to get well in a naturally unfolding, unpressured, and unpanicked growth process. The patient will be led to recognize that his or her worthiness is inherent, not earned by measuring up to the therapist's expectations, his or her own expectations, or God's.

Eighth, this clinical model provides a setting of trust, transference, and increased potential for the risk taking necessary to growth, and of *reduced injection of the therapist's pathology into the growth frame of the patient.* Ninth, this clinical perspective frees the therapist and patient to be usefully humorous about themselves, each other, and their pathologies and potentials. Tenth, this model enhances the patient's self-acceptance as a mortal person, a dying person in a generation of dying persons, but secured and cherished redemptively and eternally in the hand of Yahweh.

For me, the Christian enterprise of healing people holds out one additional and overriding dimension: the incomparable encouragement and delight that, though I may never see my patients again in their need and quandary, I shall with certainty celebrate with them and all the saints of God our mutual ecstasy of gratitude one great and glorious morning when faith has become sight, when we shall see reality whole and face-to-face, and know and affirm God as thoroughly as God now knows and affirms us.

9

Concluding Observations: Transference and Countertransference

THE SOURCES OF THE psychological sciences spring from antiquity. The development of the art of psychotherapy depends significantly upon the early church and its concern for and with the human psyche. That early practice, in a primitive way, integrated psychological process and Christian experience. For example, the early and intense use of the confessional, seen in the light of scripture and such early theologians as Aurelius Augustine, performed a valuable function of psychotherapeutic intervention by its confrontation with reality, catharsis, anxiety reduction regarding fear, guilt, and shame, pastoral acceptance, certification of the self, and behavior modification.

Luther favored retaining the confessional in Protestant practice. Moreover, the long history of pastoral care through the confessional in its ideal form was a primitive but sometimes very sophisticated form of guidance and counseling that had a moderate to excellently successful psychotherapeutic effect. It integrated psychological process and Christian experience. The church community's support systems, confession and certification systems, values clarification processes, identity and self-esteem clarification systems, purpose and behavior structuring systems, were all forces for psychological healing, social certification, and spiritual reinforcement.

Unfortunately, those structures and processes frequently have been transformed into destructive forces, fostering negative valuing of persons, coercion, rejection patterns, pathogenic conformity and achievement demands, and reinforcement of self-defeating dependency. It consistently

Concluding Observations

has been the heroic pastor and the specially inspirited communities of the church that have succeeded in building the kind of communion of trust and base of transference that have made holistic ministry a reality.

THE CHRISTIAN THERAPIST AND TRANSFERENCE

Transference is a priority concern in effective therapy. Without it little constructive movement can be expected. Negative transference inevitably structures the therapeutic process in detrimental ways. Positive transference establishes a base of trust in terms of which insight, affirmation, and growth become possible and resistance can be wholesomely eroded. Transference may be described as including the mutual affirmation of client and therapist while reserving affirmation from pathological behavior or feeling patterns in the patient.

The affirmation of the person as a person may be described from the patient's point of view as adoption of therapist in a number of healthful or health-neutral roles. The patient may establish a useful transference, such as adopting the therapist in the role of parent, friend, confidant, partner in the quest for health, professional counselor, family member, or loved one. The therapist may establish a useful transference by accepting the patient in a dependent role, patient role, familial role, or loved one role. Normally the process of transference moves through most of these roles during the progress of the therapeutic experience.

The essence of both positive transference and counter-transference is the mutual acceptance and certification of the personhood of the person in therapy, making possible effective transference, with the trust and certification which that effects. That process is the essence of unconditional love and grace. Whatever is effective in good transference in a given patient's need situation will be and will produce the Christian experience he or she must need at the outset, namely, acceptance of the person in need, apart from decisions regarding requirements for modification in attitude and behavior that will unfold as growth develops. Jung speaks of a kind of constructive projection essential to positive transference in which the patient accords the therapist an aura of the archetype healer. Jung believed that the projective process is as crucial to healing as the actual therapeutic strategy itself. Half of the healing effect, he thought, comes from the patient's perception of the therapist as effective healer.

Christian experience for the patient and the Christian expression for the therapist in positive and negative psychological processes depend exclusively on whether the psychological processes are managed toward genuine healing. Some guilt-ridden patients project a need to see the therapist as an authoritarian judge. Other neurotic patients need to experience confirmation of their neuroses by projecting rejection of themselves by the therapist and the therapeutic strategies. Still others need to ingratiate themselves with the therapist to prove their own self-worth or to create situations that seem to certify the patient's perceived rejection by the therapist who declines the opportunity to accept the ingratiation behavior.

There is a grave danger in the therapeutic process that the unlearned or unskilled therapist may be drawn inadvertently into these traps, thereby reinforcing the patient's pathology, rather than healing. Supporting and confirming the patient's pathology by therapeutic ineptness is the prime threat to authentic Christian experience in therapy, to the degree that the ineptness is unwholesome psychological process for the patient.

Similarly, in circumstances in which a patient accords the therapist a projected role of approval, acceptance, and certification of pathological behavior when the therapist intended only acceptance and certification of the person as person, unhealthful psychological process obstructs constructive Christian experience or growth.

Moreover, since therapists also may be pathological in needs and relationships, obstructive psychological processes also may emanate from therapists. Projecting a patient into a role necessary to fulfill the therapist's pathological or non-therapeutic needs, such as acceptance of counterproductive patient dependency upon the therapist or acceptance of the patient's ingratiating role, obstructs Christian growth in the manner and degree that it is psychologically counterproductive. A truly Christian caring therapist is repeatedly involved in transference and projection relationships in which the distinction between the wholesome Christian process of unconditional love and the other potentially damaging psychological process is difficult to keep clear.

It is simplistic denial to rationalize such a predicament as a Platonic relationship. There are no Platonic relationships, that is, nonsexual relationships. All relationships, wholesome or unwholesome, in therapy or out of it, are sexual in some significant dimension. We are all aware at any given moment of the maleness or femaleness of the person next to us.

On the other hand, certain forms of role identification, transference, and projection are apparently therapeutically relevant and helpful to the healing process, and contribute to the Christian model of therapy. The therapist's perception of the patient in a parent-child or in a partnership role, at certain stages of the therapy may be Christian insofar as it is productive of healing.

THE CHRISTIAN THERAPIST AND RESISTANCE

In a very general sense all psychoses, except those chemically induced, may be discussed as being the result of subconscious "decisions" for escape from pain and the mystification of reality. This amounts to an escape into a "sick world." Moreover, inhibitions, denial, depressive response to inexpressible anger, ambivalence, unidentified or inappropriate anxiety, masking, and excessive verbal stimulation are psychological processes that defend against the need to deal with internal or external reality. Hence they defend against health.

The Christian therapist's experience of the patient and the Christian role of the therapist depend upon the willingness to risk pursuit of the patient's psychological needs rather than "wants." Too often sympathy and sentimentality have been accepted by the Christian therapist as the unconditional love response to the defensive pathologies of the patient. Sympathy and sentiment are not distinctively Christian expressions and can never substitute for genuine psychological empathy and the confrontation of the patient's defensive postures. Love is usually tough stuff. If the defensive strategies are sympathetically reinforced or approved, or are not critically confronted, health and growth, psychologically and spiritually are impossible.

In sum, what is Christian in these matters is what works psychologically, since unconditional love is the pursuit, at all cost, of what heals the needy human and enhances growth. Psychological growth and growth in Christian experience differ in specific ways, but they move toward the same objective of the totally complete and fulfilled person.

THE CHRISTIAN THERAPIST AND THERAPEUTIC REALISM

Coping with realism as a Christian patient or therapist requires acknowledgement of the crucial fact that Christian psychotherapy must be kept distinct from Christian moralization. Christian morals are crucial to personality health and fulfillment, but the psychotherapeutic process is to be conditioned by the strategies that bring that health to this patient in his or her present state of illness and need, not by strategies designed to defend Christian moral structure as the primary objective.

Since unconditional love is the Christian process of people-care and since sympathy, sentimentalism, and moralization are escapes from exercising that love, the Christian therapist must insist that only good scientific psychology can become Christian therapy. Confrontation of and coping with reality in Christian psychotherapy requires those conditions in which the therapist's patient-acceptance is of such a nature as to afford the patient self-acceptance precisely in his or her mental illness predicament.

That in turn will produce the conditions in which the patient is empowered to accept the reality intrinsic and extrinsic to himself or herself in those terms necessary to the health and stability appropriate to change and development in the patient's life. There is a discernible interaction between experiencing God's unconditional acceptance, experiencing the therapist's transference of acceptance, and experiencing the ability to accept and change oneself as patient and person.

THE CHRISTIAN THERAPIST AND DEVOTIONAL TOOLS

Legitimate techniques for achieving the relief of God's unconditional grace and of the Christian's healthy response of saying, "If God feels like that about me, I want to be his kind of person," may include bibliotherapy. That is, therapy may sometimes include conveying to the patient some biblical information necessary to really appreciate the message of divine grace. It may be necessary and appropriate to include this in the psychotherapy process, not as a substitute for sound scientific psychotherapy, but as a way of fixing the needed insight in the patient that makes for the wholeness that the relief of grace brings.

The danger of this process is that the Christian structures and affirmations become the primary process and that sound psychotherapeutic process becomes its assistant. That is generally counterproductive to psychotherapy. Moreover, the essential nature of a large percentage of psychopathologies which distort and confuse the lives of patients, especially those that involve a mix of sexual and spiritual disorders, are such that psychotherapeutic techniques that are primarily "Christian guidance" play right into the patient's disorders. This is sure to reinforce the religious

Concluding Observations

and psychic distortions instead of healing them. This is especially true with various forms of psychosis and schizophrenia.

When a patient has achieved some healthful level of realism and self-acceptance, development of some wholesome aspects of the Christian life and world view may be possible, together with progress to an appropriate devotional life of spiritual experience and religious practices. Presumably such a pattern of Christian perception, perspective, and function would include all levels of personality function: social-psychological, religious, and spiritual. That makes possible a life of trust instead of fear, self-acceptance instead of perfectionism, and self-forgiveness and humility instead of self-righteousness and denial. The Christian way of life will also produce health manifestations such as (a) prayer, worship, and liturgy experience as celebration of grace and not as manipulation of God; (b) honest rationality and mysticism; (c) humanness instead of supernaturalism; and therefore, (d) incarnation theology instead of magical theology.

Healthy persons and healthy Christian persons, in short, are those who have achieved sufficient integrity, useful contact with reality, honest touch with their feeling world, sufficient awareness of the tentativeness of all human perception, and a free dynamic rather than static state of life. Such a state indicates that the person has achieved a perspective about self and others, a certainty about God's infinite grace, and a celebration of the Christian way, which leads to authenticity.

It is difficult to assess how directive a therapist can afford to be regarding the use of prayer, worship, confession of sin, or profession of faith in all of this. Surely the Christian therapist will feel an authentic need for treating the patient holistically until the patient arrives at a complete sense of meaning, motivation, and appropriate Christian behavior. However suggestions for achieving that completion may go beyond necessities of functional psychological health. Then, perhaps they should be dealt with as a stage of care beyond psychotherapy. Such Christian spiritual caring is appropriate to the therapist-patient relationship, even if in a specific case it is not appropriate to the therapy itself. The role of an effective church congregation as a support community often proves most helpful in this regard.

Religious techniques are dangerous in therapy, not because they lack affinity to scientific psychology or the discrete work of psychotherapy, but because these religious phenomena so readily play into the pathology of the patient *or of the therapist*. That does not mean that these techniques should be forbidden or eliminated. It means that they should be included in the therapy only in a setting in which the therapist has satisfactorily discerned that there are no pathologies into which such spiritual emphases or religious activities will play, pathologically. The Christian way for a Christian therapist to treat a Christian patient whose religious practices are of such a distorted nature or effect as to reinforce or even create his pathological dysfunction is to urge that patient to eliminate those religious practices.

I once treated a patient that was intensely obsessive-compulsive. This pathology prevented the patient from having a normal daily routine that permitted him to do his work and carry on normally at home. One of the chief expressions of his disorder was his belief that he should follow a ritual of prayer for himself and all those around him many times each hour. He felt that this was especially important as a means to deliver him from his obsessive compulsivity. After discerning the real nature of his disorder and establishing a trusted rapport with the poor fellow, I suggested to him a treatment plan that required both therapeutic catharsis and some changes in his behavior, if that was possible. I told him that it would be important to the therapy that he stop praying for one month. I used Christ's words to assure him that God knows what he needs before he prayed and God would help in the healing without his obsessive attempts to talk God into doing important things for him, which God would not have the good sense or presence of mind to do if he did not talk God into it.

Initially he was very shocked that I, a Christian therapist, told him he should stop praying. Eventually, with the assistance of medication and cultivating a model of trust in me and in God, he came progressively to release his need for his obsessive religious behavior. He came to see it as a psychological pathology and not a religious phenomenon.

The healthy Christian is intended to be at least wholesome and whole in his psyche, even if not unusually religious. Psychological health and Christian life require at least spiritual freedom, even if his or her processes of Christian life and discipline may not as yet be mature, and growth not yet complete.

Afterword

IN 1970 J. HAROLD Ellens delivered the prestigious Finch Commemorative Lectures at Fuller Graduate School of Psychology. His series of lectures were a stirring challenge calling for a new initiative in the interface and integration of theology and psychology. His goal was to create a model for producing responsible Christian psychotherapy. Those lectures were presented to scholarly audiences in various ways at conferences and in published papers. A small monograph called *God's Grace and Human Health* of those papers was privately distributed to a few close acquaintances and students. The response was extraordinarily enthusiastic.

It is of great significance, therefore, that Dr. Ellens has now prepared this scholarly volume of theory and practice for the interested and informed reader. Typical of Dr. Ellens' books, it is written for both the layperson and the professional. It incorporates the essence of the Finch lectures and expands that to comprehend the larger matter of spelling out engagingly the roots and grounds, as well and the model and spirit of Christian Psychotherapy. This is one of the most significant contributions on the contemporary perspective on the integration of psychology and Christian theology, religion, and spirituality. His title, *Science, Religion, and Health* is articulate and thus well-chosen.

In the atrium of Fuller Graduate School of Psychology, where I held the Integration Chair until my retirement, there stands a sculpture of a life-size cross into which is embedded the Greek letter Psi, the symbol for psychology. Below it is inscribed the poignant words, *Putting Christ in the Heart of Psychology*.

The historical memory is that these were words of John G. Finch, expressed at the founding of the Graduate School of Psychology. Ellens has given that inspired statement wings with this volume of erudite dialogue on the foundations of the Jewish/Christian doctrine of God's radical, unconditional, and universal grace, as articulated in God's Covenant of Grace with Abraham at Genesis 12 and 17, and Paul's expression of Jesus' message in Romans 8.

He grounds his work in the claim that the origin of our religious impulse lies in human anxiety.

Our anxiety is born of our finitude. We are born extremely fragile into an unknown world. We remain aware of our finitude all our lives. We feel like we are "cast out of the paradise of the womb and cannot quite catch hold of our father's hand." I only recently became aware of how pervasive such anxiety is and how important it is to face it rather than live in denial of it. You have heard of the citizens of the Asian country of Bhutan which is described as the "happiest place on earth." They are taught to think at least once a day of their inevitable death. Apparently, the Bhutanese live under a philosophy that teaches them to handle their existential anxiety and finitude by daily confrontation with it, a kind of desensitization. Dealing with their finitude with intentionality as part of the daily reality affords them a day-to-day contentment.

As a clinical psychologist, Ellens has given us a volume in which he extends his understanding of the religious roots of our problem to psychotherapeutic insights for addressing this problem. While giving counsel based on theological assumptions is by no means new, the officially sanctioned role of psychologists who counsel, instead of priests and pastoral caregivers, is a product of the twentieth century. Addressing one's finitude or anxiety clinically does not cure it automatically because psychotherapists vary in their presumptions about human nature and need, and persons and their life situations are each unique. We are not all privileged to live life on the same level playing field. Psychotherapists must school themselves in various models and methods that work with the religious and psychological dynamics. Ellens' grace theology provides a sense of how the burden of life's basic anxiety can be addressed regardless of the unique form the problem takes in a given life and at what point the counselor is asked to intervene.

This sturdy volume does a worthy job of exploring the historical foundations for the basic approaches theologically informed psychologists take. These are grounded in scripture, theological traditions, and the Aristotelian or Platonic philosophy that stands behind such traditions. I should like to offer three sources that might supplement Ellens' already rich coverage of the matter. They enhance his understandings of the interrelationships of Christian theology to psychospiritual health.

Afterword

Harvard theologian Gordon Kaufman (1968) suggested that the prime fact of human existence was humans ability to make history. No other organism in God's creation can act in a way that develops historical roots. Apart from instinct or habit formation, only humans can initiate events, remember them, record them and act upon them, and thus extend them into the future. Theologically, God created humans as his co-creators. God's intention for human life is that they should join God in making this earth fulfill God's intentions. That is the process of making history come to pass. Love is the overarching goal; justice and unselfishness are an important rule. Jesus exemplified this and calls humans to follow in his footsteps. For a psychotherapist to help people overcome their anxiety is to assist them to adopt that kind of life in whatever unique situation they find themselves. Life is to be accepted as a time-limited period in which the prime goal should be to contribute a part to God's will for creation, including our own wellbeing. Kaufman's historicist perspective fits well with Ellens' "compatriot" model for a therapeutic goal.

Similarly, Samuel Southard (1989) considers psychotherapy within the context of friendship understood as "the context for communication of the wisdom of God under special circumstances" (201). While Ellens deals largely with the *content* of psychotherapy, Southard focuses on the *context*. He proposes that in sharing wisdom there are some striking differences from secular therapy. First, there is an open dedication to a godly mission. There is a sense of worship in the conversation. This should be explicit, not assumed.

Secondly, there is an awareness that the source of the wisdom sought by therapist and patient lies beyond both of them. The presence of God is the context of the therapy. They acknowledge their essential equality in the search for health and wholeness. Both therapist and client are at worship. Both are seeking the will of God for life. Moreover, they entrust themselves to the support of the body of Christ (the church), that stands behind the organization that sponsors the therapy. Southard defines wisdom-seeking as "loving within limits." He defines "friendship" similarly. Christian wisdom "works among us as created beings, moving from friendship toward the universal love of God" (203).

Finally, the reasoning of Gary W. Deddo (1999) supplements Ellens work nicely while interpreting Karl Barth. He does not deal with the *interface* of psychology with theology. Nor does he discuss any of the dimensions of therapeutic counseling. He is primarily concerned with a Christological discussion of human relations that could be a way of understanding the meaning of the statement on the statue of Fuller's atrium *Putting Christ in the Heart of Psychology*. To put Christ in the heart of psychology would mean a radically "Trinitarian" interpretation of the personhood of Jesus of Nazareth. Barth contends that the "trinity" was not simply proposed to understand God after the appearance of Jesus, followed by a Holy Spirit. Barth proposes that God was a "trinity" of Father/Son/Spirit from the beginning as implied in John 1:1ff. Jesus is appropriately labeled the *Son of God*. As such, Christ is the model we should aspire to every way. Barth reportedly said "Christ is who we are."

The implications of this are many, for Ellens' postulate of our being co-laborers with Christ in God's vineyard throughout our lives, compatriots of God as it were. Barth's radical understanding should not be missed. He contends that any life that is lived apart from a sense of being identified with Christ is, by definition, sin. We were made to be like Christ. This does not mean "everyone is Christ." We are created, not cloned. It identifies for us what the goal of life is, and what therapeutic counseling should be.

Reading Ellens' new volume is an enticing, informative, and inspirational experience, with or without these additions.

H. Newton Malony
Professor Emeritus of Pschyology
Fuller Theological Seminary, School of Psychology

Bibliography

Allen, Reginald E., ed. 1966 *Greek Philosophy: Thales to Aristotle*, New York: Free Press-Macmillan.
Arapura, J. G. 1973. *Religion as Anxiety and Tranquility*. Paris: Mouton.
Barth, Karl. 1957. *The Epistle to the Romans*. Kindle edition, 2016. Oxford: Oxford University Press.
———. 2010. *Church Dogmatics*. Peabody, MA: Hendricksen.
Beker, J. Christiaan. 1980. *Paul the Apostle: The Triumph of God in Life and Thought*. Philadelphia: Fortress.
Berry, C. Markham. 1980a. Approaching the Integration of the Social Sciences and Biblical Theology, *JPT* 8:1 (Spring).
———. 1980b. Entering Canaan: Adolescence as a Stage of Spiritual Growth. *The Bulletin of CAPS* 6:4.
Betz, Hans Dieter. 1985. *2 Corinthians 8 and 9*. Hermeneia. Minneapolis: Fortress.
———. 1989. *Galatians*. Hermeneia. Minneapolis: Fortress.
Blanton, Smiley, and Edward Robinson. 1957. *Love or Perish*. New York: Simon & Schuster.
Bloesch, Donald. 2010. *God, the Almighty*. New York: Academic Press.
Blum, H. L. 1974. *Planning for Health: Developmental Application of Social Change Theory*. New York: Human Sciences Press.
Boisen, Anton. 1971. *Exploration of the Inner World: A Study of Mental Disorder and Religious Experience*. Philadelphia: University of Pennsylvania Press.
———. 2015. *Out of the Depths: An Autobiographical Study of Mental Disorder and Religious Experience*. New York: Harper.
Boghasian, Jack. 1980. Theology Recapitulates Ontogeny: Reality Testing as an Analog in Relating to God. *JPT* 8:2 (Summer).
Boman, Thorleif. 1960. *Hebrew Thought Compared with Greek*. Jules L. Moreau, (tr), New York: Norton.
Bratton, F. G. 1970. *Myths and Legends of the Ancient Near East*. New York: Crowell.
Brister, C. W. 1964. *Pastoral Care in the Church*. New York: Harper & Row.
Bromiley, Geoffrey W. 1960. *Christian Ministry*. Grand Rapids: Eerdmans.
Bry, Adelaide. 1973. *The TA Primer*. New York: Harper & Row.
Bube, Richard H. 1971. Toward a Christian View of Science. *JASA* 32:4.
———. 1976. *The Human Quest*. Waco: Word Books.
Bufford, Rodger. 1980. Christian Counseling: Issues and Trends. *The Bulletin of CAPS* 6:4.
Bulfinch, Thomas. 1959. *Bulfinch's Mythology*. Abbreviated edition edited by Edmund Fuller. New York: Dell.
Burn, A. R. 1983. *The Pelican History of Greece*. Baltimore: Penguin.

Bibliography

Burnet, John. 1958. *Early Greek Philosophy*. New York: New American Library (Meridian).
Capps, Donald. 2000. *Jesus: A Psychological Biography*. Reprinted, Eugene, OR: Wipf & Stock, 2010.
———. 2008. *Jesus, The Village Psychiatrist*. Louisville: Westminster John Knox.
Childs, Brevard. 1979. *Introduction to the Old Testament as Scripture*. Harrisburg: Fortress.
Clebsch, William A., and Charles R. Jaekle. 1975. *Pastoral Care in Historical Perspective*. New York: Aronson.
Clement, Paul W., and Niel C. Warren. 1973. "Can Religion and Psychotherapy Be Happily Married? An Experiment in Education." In *Religious Systems and Psychotherapy*, edited by R. H. Cox, 417–26. Springfield, IL: Thomas.
Clifford, P. R. 1961. *The Pastoral Calling*. New York: Channel.
Clinebell, Howard J. 1979. *Growth Counseling: Hope Centered Methods of Actualizing Human Wholeness*. Nashville: Abingdon.
———. 1984. *Basic Types of Pastoral Counseling*. Rev. ed. Nashville: Abingdon.
Clines, David J. A. 1968. "The Image of God in Man." *Tyndale Bulletin* 19:53–103.
Cochrane, Charles N. 2003. *Christianity and Classical Culture: A Study of Thought and Action from Augustus to Augustine*. New York: Oxford University Press.
Collins, Gary. 1977. *The Rebuilding of Psychology*. Wheaton, IL: Tyndale House.
Cooper, Lane. 2016. *Greek Genius and Its Influence*. Ithaca, NY: Leopold Classics Library.
Cornford, F. M. 1972. *Before and After Socrates*. New York: Cambridge University Press.
———. 2010. *Plato's Theory of Knowledge*. New York: Routledge.
Cryer, N. S. Jr., and John M. Vayhinger, eds. 1962. *Casebook in Pastoral Counseling*. Nashville: Abingdon.
Daane, James. 1973. *The Freedom of God*. Grand Rapids: Eerdmans.
Daiches, David, Anthony Thorlby, eds. 1972. *The Classical World Literature and Western Civilization*. Vol. 1. London: Aldus.
De Graaf. Arnold H. 1980. "Toward an Integral Model of Psychotherapy." *The Bulletin of CAPS* 6:3.
Deddo, Gary W. 1999. *Karl Barth's Theology of Relations: Trinitarian, Christological, and Human. Towards an Ethic of the Family* . Issues in Systematic Theology 4. New York, NY: Lang.
The Detroit Magazine. *Detroit Free Press*. April 14, 1974.
Dever, G. E. Alan. 1976. "An Epidemiological Model for Health Policy Analysis." In *Social Indicators Research*. Dordrecht: Reidel.
Dicks, Russell L. 2011. *Pastoral Work and Personal Counseling*. New York: Macmillan.
———. 1980. *Toward Health and Wholeness*. New York: Macmillan.
Dubos, René. 1974. *Beast or Angel? Choices That Make Us Human*. New York: Scribner.
Eliade, Mircea. 2009. *Immortality and Freedom*. Translated by Willard R. Trask. New York: Pantheon.
———. 1959. *Cosmos and History*. Translated by Willard R. Trask. New York: Harper.
Ellens, J. Harold. 1974. "A Theology of Communication." *JPT* 2:2.
———. 1974. "Anxiety and Religion." *CAPS Proceedings*.
———. 1975. "Anxiety and the Rise of Religious Experience." *JPT* 3:1.
———. 1976. "Psychological Process and Christian Experience in Psychotherapy." In *Research in Mental Health and Religious Behavior*, edited by William J. Donaldson Jr., ed. Atlanta: Psychological Studies Institute.
———. 1980. "Biblical Themes in Psychological Theory and Practice." *The Bulletin of CAPS* 6:2.

Bibliography

———. 2007. *Radical Grace: How Belief in a Benevolent God Benefits Our Health*. Westport, CT: Praeger.

———. 2008. *Understanding Religious Experience: What the Bible Says about Spirituality*. Westport, CT: Praeger.

———. 2012. *A Dangerous Report, Challenging Sermons for Advent and Easter*. Newcastle, UK: Cambridge Scholars.

———. 2012. *God's Radical Grace: Challenging Sermons for Ordinary Time(s)*. Newcastle, UK: Cambridge Scholars.

———. 2013. *By Grace Alone: Forgiveness for Everyone, for Everything, for Evermore*. Eugene, OR: Wipf & Stock.

———. eds. 2014. *Seeking the Sacred with Psychoactive Substances: Chemical Paths to Spirituality and to God*. Santa Barbara, CA: Praeger.

Ellis, Peter. 1968. *The Yahwist: The Bible's First Theologian*. Notre Dame: Fides.

Farnsworth, Kirk. 1974. "Embodied Integration." *JPT* 2:2.

Feder, Lillian. 1980. *Crowell's Handbook of Classical Literature*. San Francisco: HarperCollins.

Ferguson, John. 1975. *Utopias of the Classical World*. Aspects of Greek and Roman Life. Ithaca, NY: Cornell University Press.

Fleck, J. Roland, and John D. Carter. 1981. *Psychology and Christianity: Integrative Readings*. Nashville: Abingdon.

Frankl, Viktor E. 1963. *Man's Search for Himself*. New York, NY: Washington Square.

———. 1986. *The Doctor and the Soul*. 2nd ed. Translated by Richard and Clare Winston. London: Souvenir.

———. 2014. *Man's Search for Meaning*. Boston: Beacon.

Frazer, James George. 2002. *The Golden Bough*. Abr. ed. Mineola, NY: Dover.

Freud, Sigmund. 2013. *New Introductory Lectures on Psychoanalysis*. Edited and translated by James Stracey. New York, NY: Martino Fine Books.

Fromm, Eric. 1910. *The Heart of Man: Its Genius for Good and Evil*. New York, NY: Lantern.

———. 1970. *Psychoanalysis and Religion*. New York, NY: Bantam.

———. 1997. *The Anatomy of Human Destructiveness*. New York, NY: Pimlico.

Gaster, Theodor. 1975. *Myth, Legend, and Custom in the Old Testament*. New York, NY: Harper & Row.

Golden, Harry. 1960. *Enjoy! Enjoy!* New York, NY: World.

Grant, Michael. 1988. *The Ancient Mediteranean*. New York, NY: Plume.

Guthrie, W. K. C. 1965. *In the Beginning: Some Greek Views on the Origins of Life and the Early State of Man*. Ithaca, NY: Cornell University Press.

———. 2000. *The History of Greek Philosophy*. Vols. 1–6. Cambridge: Cambridge University Press.

Hall, Calvin S. 2011. *A Primer of Freudian Psychology*. New York, NY: Literary Licensing.

Hall, Calvin S., and Gardner Lindzey. 1978. *Theories of Personality*. New York, NY: Wiley.

Hamilton, Edith. 1993. *The Roman Way*. New York, NY: Norton.

———. 2010. *The Greek Way*. New York, NY: Norton.

Harriman, P. L. 2006. *The New Dictionary of Psychology*. New York, NY: Wiley.

Hiltner, Seward. 1949. *Pastoral Counseling*. Nashville: Abingdon.

Hiltner, Seward, and Karl Menninger, eds. 1963. *Constructive Aspects of Anxiety*, Nashville: Abingdon.

Holmes, Arthur Frank. 1971. *Faith Seeks Understanding: A Christian Approach to Knowledge*. Grand Rapids: Eerdmans.

Bibliography

———. 1977. *All Truth is God's Truth*. Downers Grove, IL: InterVarsity.
Horney, Karen. 1994. *The Neurotic Personality of Our Time*. New York, NY: Norton.
Jaeger, Werner. 1945. *Paideia: The Ideals of Greek Culture*. Vols. 1–2. Translated by Gilbert Highet. New York: Oxford University Press. Reprinted by Cultu(Bookos.org), 2013.
Jaki, Stanley L. 1978. *The Road of Science and the Ways to God*. Chicago: University of Chicago Press.
———. 1980. *Cosmos and Creator*. Ann Arbor: University of Michigan.
James, William. 2009. *Varieties of Religious Experience: A Study in Human Nature*. CreateSpace Independent Publishing Platform. First published in 1911 in London: Longmans Green Ltd.
Johnson, Paul E. 1959. *Psychology of Religion*. Nashville: Abingdon.
Jung, Carl G. 1958. *The Undiscovered Self*. Translated by R. F. C. Hull. Boston: Little, Brown.
———. 1964. *Man and His Symbols*. Garden City, NY: Doubleday.
———. 1966. *Psychology and Religion*. New Haven: Yale University Press.
Kauffman, Gordon. 1968. *Systematic Theology: A Historicist Perspective*. New York, NY: Charles Scribner and Sons.
Kierkegaard, Søren. 1954. *Fear and Trembling/The Sickness unto Death*. Translated byWalter Lowrie. Garden City, NY: Doubleday.
———. 1957. *The Concept of Dread*. Translated by Walter Lowrie. Princeton: Princeton University Press.
Koteskey, Ronald L. 1980. *Psychology from a Christian Perspective*. Nashville: Abingdon.
Lalonde, M. 1974. *A New Perspective on the Health of Canadians*. Ottawa: Office of the Canadian Minister of National Health and Welfare.
Linn, Louis, and Leo Schwarz. 1958. *Psychiatry and Religious Experience*. New York, NY: Random House.
Locke, John. 1977. *The Locke Reader: Selections from the Works of John Locke*. Edited by John Yolton. Cambridge: Cambridge University Press.
MacKay, Donald. 1974. *The Clock Work Image: A Christian Perspective on Science*. Downers Grove, IL: InterVarsity.
Maddi, Salvatore, ed. 1996. *Personality Theories: A Comparative Analysis*. New York, NY: Cole.
Maslow, Abraham. 1992. *Motivation and Personality*. New York, NY: Harper.
May, Rollo. 1996. *Psychology and the Human Dilemma*. New York, NY: Norton.
———. 2015. *The Meaning of Anxiety*. New York. NY: Norton.
McLemore, Clinton W. 1976. "The Nature of Psychotheology: Varieties of Conceptual Integration." *JPT* 4:3.
McNeill, Robert. 1975. *God Wills Us Free*. New York, NY: Norton.
Mertz, Barbara. 2009. *Red Land, Black Land*. 2nd ed. New York, NY: Morrow.
Morford, Mark P. O., and Robert J. Lenardon. 2013. *Classical Mythology*. 10th ed. Oxford: Oxford University Press.
Morris, J. N. 1975. *Uses of Epidemiology*. 3rd ed. Edinburgh: Churchill Livingstone.
Murray, Gilbert. 2010. *Five Stages of Greek Religion*. New York, NY: CreativeSpace. Independent Publishing Platform.
Nouwen, Henri. 1990. *The Wounded Healer*. Garden City, NY: Doubleday.
Oates, Wayne. 1974. *Pastoral Counseling*. Lousville: Westminster John Knox.
Orlebeke, Clifton J. 1977. "Donald MacKay's Philosophy of Science." *Christian Scholars Review* 7:1.
Ornstein, Robert E. 1986. *The Psychology of Consciousness*. New York, NY: Penguin.

Bibliography

Otto, Rudolf. 2010. *The Idea of the Holy*. New York, NY: Martino.
Outler, Albert. 1997. *The Pastoral Psychology of Albert Cook Outler*. New York, NY: Bristol House.
Punt, Niel. 1980. *Unconditional Good News: Towards an Understanding of Biblical Universalism*. Grand Rapids: Eerdmans.
Rand, Ayn. 1964. *The Virtue of Selfishness*, New York: Signet.
Restak, Richard M. 1988. *The Brain, the Last Frontier*. New York: Grand Central Publishing.
Ridderbos, Herman. 1997. *Paul, An Outline of His Theology*. Grand Rapids: Eerdmans.
Rogers, Carl. 1965. *Client Centered Therapy*. New York, NY: Houghton Miflin.
Ruch, Floyd L., and Philip G. Zimbardo. 1988. *Psychology and Life*. 12th ed. New York, NY: Longman.
Rusestam, Arvid. 1958. *Psychoanalysis and Christianity*. Rev. ed. Translated by Oscar Winfield. Rock Island, IL: Augustana.
Ryan, Regina, and John Travis, M.D. 1981. *Wellness Workbook*. San Francisco: Ten-Speed Press.
Schaefer, Francis A. 2001. *True Spirituality*. Wheaton, IL: Tyndale.
———. 2007. *Escape from Reason*. Downers Grove: InterVarsity
Schleiermacher, Friedrich, 2011, *The Christian Faith*, New York, NY: Apocryphile Press.
Schuurman, Egbert. 1980. *Reflection on the Technological Society*, Toronto: Wedge.
———. 2009. *Technology and the Future: A Philosophical Challenge*, Philadelphia: Paideia.
Seligman, Martin E. P. 2002, *Authentic Happiness, Using the New Positive Psychology to Realize Your Potential for Lasting Fulfillment*. New York, NY: Simon & Schuster.
———. 2006. *Learned Optimism: How to Change Your Mind and Your Life*. New York, NY: Vintage.
———. 2012. *Flourishing: A New Understanding of Happiness and Well Being*. Philadelphia: Atria.
Shattuck, Lemuel 1850. *Report on the Sanitary Conditions in the State of Massachusetts*. Boston: Dutton & Wentworth, State Printers, No. 37 Congress Street.
Siegler, Miriam, and Humphrey Osmond. 1974. *Models of Madness, Models of Medicine*. New York: Macmillan.
Simon, Bennett. 1984. *Mind and Madness in Ancient Greece*, Ithaca: Cornell University Press.
Singer, June. 1994. *Boundaries of the Soul: The Practice of Jung's Psychology*. Garden City, NY: Doubleday.
Southard, Samuel. 1989. *Theology and Therapy: The Wisdom of God in a Context of Friendship*. Pasadena: Western Publishing Group.
Standal, Stanley, and Raymond J. Corsini. 1959. *Critical Incidents in Psychotherapy*. Englewood Cliffs, NJ: Prentice Hall.
Thornton, Edward E. 1970. *Theology and Pastoral Counseling*. 2nd ed. Philadelphia: Fortress.
Tillich, Paul. 1957. *The Meaning of Persons*. Translated by Edwin Hudson. New York, NY: Harper.
Tournier, Paul. 1982. *Guilt and Grace: A Psychological Study*. Translated by Arthur W. Heathcote. New York, NY: Harper & Row.
Weatherhead, Leslie D. 2007. *Psychology, Religion, and Healing*. New York, NY: Stewart.
White, Robert W. 1956. *Abnormal Personality*. New York, NY: Ronald.
Williams, J. F. 1946. *Personal Hygiene Applied*. 8th ed. Philadelphia: Saunders.
Wolterstorff, Nicholas, 1976, *Reason Within the Bounds of Religion*. Grand Rapids: Eerdmans.

Index

Adam, 64, 70ff
Adler, 12, 36
Allport, 36
Alternative Medicine, 5
Anthropology, 30, 31, 38, 82, 87ff, 93ff, 100ff
Anxiety, 40, 59, 60, 71ff
Aquinas, Thomas, 32
Arapura, J. G., 42
Aristotle, 4, 32, 34, 112
Asklepios, 3
Augustine, Aurelius, 18, 34

Bacon, Francis, 32
Barth, Karl, 66, 113ff
Beker, J. Christiaan, 66
Berry, C. Markham, 72ff
Betz, Hans Dieter, 65, 83ff
Bible, 49, 50, 52, 54, 59, 68, 69
Biology, 8, 100
Bloesch, Donald, 66
Blum, H. L., 7
Boisen, Anton, 72ff
Borman, Thorlief, 32

Capps, Donald, 12
Childs, Brevard S., 55
Clinebell, Howard J., 72ff
Clines, David, J. A., 63
Daane, James, 66
Deddo, Gary W., 113
Delphi, 83ff
Dever, G. E. Alan, 8
Documentary Hypothesis, x
Drewermann, Eugen, 12

Ecology, 6, 7
Education, 7, 9
Egyptians, 2, 44
Eliade, Mircea, 45, 46
Ellis, Albert, 36, 99
Entheogens, 6
Environment, 6, 7, 8
Environmental Psychology, 5
Epidemiology, 6, 8
Evangelical, 15, 101
Experience, 6, 39, 40, 41
Extrinsic Forces, 6

Faculty Psychology, 5
Fall, 57, 64, 68ff
Finch, John G., 56, 111
Forgiveness, 21
Fowler, James, 12
Frankl, Victor, 12
Frazer, James George, 40
Freud, Sigmund, 5, 12, 35
Fromm, Eric, 12, 36, 56
Fundamentalism, 13, 28, 52, 101

Galen, 3
Gene Pool, 7
Genetics, 6, 8
Goethe, Johann von, 92
Golden, Harry, 45
Grace, 19, 27, 44, 47, 62, 65, 66, 67, 92, 100ff, 111
Great Society, 5
Greek, 2, 3, 11, 32, 33, 34, 81, 84ff
Growth, 7, 9, 93

Index

Hall, Calvin S., 37
Health, 1, 2, 3, 4, 7, 8, 10, 12, 59, 65, 94ff, 100
Health Care Services, 7, 8
Health Field Concept, 7, 8, 105
Hebrew, 2, 32, 33, 34, 54, 68, 69, 73, 76, 81, 84ff
Hegel, George Friedrisch, 83
Heredity, 7
Hermeneutics, 50
Hiltner, Seward, 41
Hippocrates, 3
Holmes, Arthur, 12, 14
Holy Spirit, 13, 15
Hope, 58
Horney, Karen, 42

Integration, 12, 29
Intrinsic Forces, 6

Jaki, Stanley L. 28
James, William, 12
Jesus of Nazareth, 48, 92
Johnson, L. B., 5
Jung, Carl, 12, 21, 35, 41, 47

Kaufman, Gordon, 113
Kennedy, J. F., 5
Kierkegaard, Søren, 45

Lacan, Jacques, 12
Lalonde, M., 8
Lindzey, Gardner, 37
Living Human Document, 14
Locke, John, 3

Maddi, Salvadore R., 34, 35, 38
Madness, 11
Maslow, Abraham, 12, 36, 38, 99.
Maturation, 8, 94ff
Mertz, Barbara, 44
Mesopotamia, 2, 68, 81ff
Mind, 6, 11
Morris, J. N., 6
Mysticism, 52

Near East, 2
Nouwen, Henri, 21
Nous, 9

Oates, Wayne, 101
Occult, 9
Otto, Rudolf, 45
Osmond, Humphrey, 96ff
Outler, Albert C., 43

Perls, Fritz, 35
Personality Theory, 35
Pharmacology, 6
Piaget, Jean, 12
Pneuma, 9
Positive Psychology, 33
Preaching, ix, x
Psyche, 6, 78
Psychedelic Substances, 6
Psychology, ix, 10, 12, 13, 15, 16, 26, 27, 29, 30, 31, 32, 37, 45, 49, 50, 53, 58, 67, 68, 94, 100ff, Psychology, 13
Psychotheology, 94ff, 102ff, 113
Psychotherapy, 2, 14, 23, 38, 93ff, 100, 106ff, 111
Punt, Niel, 66

Qur'an, 15

Rank, Otto, 35
Religion, 11, 40, 42, 61
Restak, Robert, 34
Ridderbos, Herman, 89, 91
Rogers, Carl, 12, 36, 37, 67, 99ff
Roman, 2, 3
Ryan, Regina, 9

Schuurman, Egbert, 27
Science, 11, 14, 29, 30
Self Image, 5
Seligman, Martin, 12, 33, 36, 37
Shattuck, A. M. 2
Siegler, Miriam, 96
Simon, Bennett, 11
Sin, 20, 56
Social Ecological Model, 6
Social Psychology, 5
Southard, Samuel, 113
Spiritual Health, x, 10
Spirituality, 11, 12, 24, 50, 52, 53

Index

Theology, 10, 11, 12, 19, 20, 21, 25, 26, 27, 29, 30, 31, 32, 37, 54, 94ff, 101ff
Theory, 29, 30, 31
Tillich, Paul, 46
Transference, 24, 104ff
Travis, John, 9

United States, 5, 76

White, Robert W., 36
WHO, 5, 6
Williams, J. F., 4
Winnecott, Donald, 12
Wolterstorff, Nicholas, 12
Wounded Healer, 21

Yahwist, x, 17, 63, 80

Zika, 5

www.ingramcontent.com/pod-product-compliance
Lightning Source LLC
Chambersburg PA
CBHW030902170426
43193CB00009BA/709